# THE
# FAITH OF OUR
# CHILDREN

## Eight Timely Research Insights
## For Discipling The Next Generation

**MATT MARKINS**

**D6 FAMILY MINISTRY**
114 BUSH RD - NASHVILLE, TN 37217 - 800.877.7030 - D6FAMILY.COM

Published by D6 Family Ministry

ISBN: 9781614841685

# DEDICATION

To Peter Mayberry, and Norm Whitney
(who is more alive now than ever).

In a world of fast, you taught me slow.
Like an artist perfecting his craft,
your curiosity to ask the hard questions
and your thirst to keep learning
is what inspired a decade's worth of research.
Here's to the future of the Church—a church that
intentionally and thoughtfully forms the faith of children.

# TABLE OF CONTENTS

# INTRODUCTION

## After a decade of research, what have we learned about forming the faith of our children?

Watching a young person grow to adulthood isn't a miracle. It's a normal process. But it sure does *feel* like a miracle.

My sons are now 21 and 19 and I marvel at how someone who was once so vulnerable and helpless is now driving, making autonomous decisions, and managing multiple bank accounts. How did that happen? And how did that happen seemingly so quickly?!

Being a parent—or for that matter an aunt, uncle, teacher, coach, pastor, counselor, or church volunteer—can be a lot like being a master craftsman. There's a good amount of modeling, mentoring, teaching, forming, envisioning, and coaching. Along with the pain of splinters, smashed thumbs, and bruised egos, comes the joy of watching the young apprentice take that first solo step, the winning RBI, the stellar dance performance, the High School diploma, and the *how has this happened so quickly?* feeling when they drive away to college.

What we are discussing here is *formation.*

Formation is this messy mash-up of all the little mundane moments that get connected to all of the highs and lows that build the little persons into big persons. It isn't a miracle. It's normal. Bit by bit.

It's often said, "it's not a matter of are our children being discipled, but rather who or what is discipling our children?" In 2023 and beyond, a world that now includes new words in the headlines like *Splinternet, Transhumanism, ChatGPT, NFTs, and Transgenderism*, it's more clear now than ever that cultural formation is a force to be reckoned with when it comes to our children.

1

And like me, you probably spend a lot of time wondering, am I adequately preparing them?

The kids in my family...

The kids in our church...

The kids in our school system...

The kids whom we love and care about so deeply...

Will they have a resilient faith in Jesus Christ? Will they bend and flex and not break under the weight of culture? Will they love and follow Jesus in a world of hostility? Will they lead the future of the church with biblical faithfulness and Christlike compassion?

These are the things we wonder. Our sleepless nights and persistent prayers are consumed with these sorts of questions and sometimes unformed, unspeakable tear-filled longings.

Sigh. Deep breath. Lord, please help us.

## What Do We Know for Sure? And What Do We Not Know?

I'm reminded of this quote attributed to Mark Twain:

> *"It ain't what you don't know that gets you into trouble.*
> *It's what you know for sure that just ain't so."*[1]

When I first read this quote I laughed. Then the pit of my stomach filled with anxiety (Cast your cares...I know) as I thought about how we shape the future of today's children and youth. I thought about *us*. I thought about:

- Parents of infants, preschoolers, children, teens, and young adults
- Children's ministry leaders
- Teachers and coaches
- Pastors and youth pastors
- Grandparents
- Church volunteers and mentors

Every day we operate on a certain set of assumptions about how we form faith in children as young disciples. But are our assumptions correct?

When Covid-19 hit the world with full force by the Spring of 2020, there was a lot being written about our reliance upon certain systems and presupposed assumptions (prior to that point in history). Understandably! Covid caught most of us flat-footed and knocked us off balance. Our normal systems were compromised. It was the prime opportunity to pause, reflect, and ask questions.

This is precisely what happened. Many churches—in some way—adapted and pivoted to press forward in the ministry of the Gospel as a result of some level of discussion, debate, reflection, and assessment of: What do we do now? Why do we do it the way we do it? What is the most faithful and fruitful way to do this going forward?

Although this season was challenging, it was good for the church. It caused the church to ask *real* questions and, in some cases, *hard* questions. As with the quote attributed to Mark Twain, we discovered that some things we thought were absolutely certain about *how* the faith of children is formed, are just not so.

**This Is a Book About Research – One Question and Two Themes:**

We have a saying at Awana (the organization where I serve and lead), "We didn't anticipate Covid, but we did anticipate the things that Covid revealed." This is the case for us because we've been researching for quite some time prior to 2020. Our team has commissioned eleven studies in the space that is called "children's ministry" or "child discipleship." Nine of those studies are complete and two are in-process as of the time of this writing. The overarching question we've been asking in each of our research projects is this:

*"What is it the church does that leads to lasting faith in children?"*[2]

The motivation behind this question has to do with biblical faithfulness, stewardship of orthodoxy, and formational fruitfulness. Our aim is to gain and share maximum insight as to how we (the broader church community) can most faithfully maximize and steward our discipleship investment in children. If we can become more fruitful as disciple-makers, then we can reach and disciple more children for the Kingdom of God—no matter the cultural context.

Over the course of the past ten years as we've perused to answer that question, we've learned a lot. Our chief findings can be grouped into two primary themes:

1. **Formation** – The primary investments that tend to form lasting faith in children

2. **Systems** – The norms, processes, infrastructure, and culture we depend upon to form the faith of our children

As I look back over the insights we've gleaned from these projects the last decade, the wit and insight of Mark Twain rings true, "...It's what you know for sure that just ain't so."

On one hand, there is such hope in what we do know (and there's a lot we _do_ know!). This book is filled with hope about how to influence the faith formation of our children. On the other hand, I grieve what we _think_ we know with such certainty, that isn't quite the case.

The aim of this book is to aid those who care deeply about children to evaluate what forms lasting faith in children and consider the effectiveness of the systems and programs we use in faith formation.

**In Part One,** we will examine the chief insights that tend to form lasting faith in children.

**In Part Two,** we will investigate how the systems we depend upon may be incongruent with our goal of forming lasting faith in children.

As you work through these chapters and do your own thinking, evaluation, and analysis, my hope is this: I hope you get to the end of this book and decide to keep going...to read it and discuss it with others. I hope you pray and seek God's abundant wisdom. I hope you and your team will dialogue together and wrestle with the changes we must make to align our systems to our goals, objectives, and the cries of our hearts. This journey could be the most important work in your lifetime. Because child discipleship is the most fruitful and strategic work of the church.

I can't think of anything more important than the faith of our children.

## Endnotes

[1] https://www.forbes.com/sites/rodgerdeanduncan/2019/05/31/what-if-what-you-think-you-know-just-aint-so/?sh=2fe2a723355e Although Mark Twain is often attributed as the source of this quote, it's widely debated as to who exactly is the original source.

[2] Barna Group, _Children's Ministry in a New Reality: Building Church Communities That Cultivate Lasting Faith_ (Los Angeles, Barna Group, 2022), 5.

# PART 1

# FORMATION

## The Primary Investments
## That Tend to Form
## Lasting Faith in Children

# CHAPTER 1

# GOAL

## Lasting Faith Is the Desired Outcome

**The single most unifying insight in our research was this: the lifelong discipleship of our children is our desired outcome.**

Let's go back to the idea alluded to in the introduction of the "normal" versus the "miraculous" as it relates to the formation of faith in our young people. To unpack this a bit more, let me use a basic illustration. In the image below, notice the big circle and the small dot.

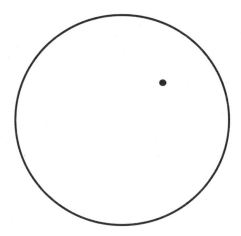

The Big Circle represents God's sovereignty (not drawn to scale, of course). God is big. He's powerful. He's all knowing...and He can do as He chooses. If He wants to part waters, He's going to do that. If He wants to multiply fish and loaves, it's done. If He wants to raise a dead man to life, it's no effort for Him. God is sovereign and has come to build His Kingdom (Exodus 14; Matthew 14; John 20; Mark 1).

The Small Dot represents human's responsibility. Although it is true that God is sovereign and He can do whatever He wants, that doesn't remove the burden of responsibility that we bear as His advocates for the Kingdom of God here on this earth. We are responsible. If we meet an injured man on the path, we respond with compassion and care. If we see trash on the sidewalk, we pick it up and throw it in the garbage. We are responsible for doing our part to disciple the people God has placed in our lives, to help them know, love, and serve the Lord Jesus Christ (Luke 10; Matthew 28).

For the Christ-follower, *this* is the framework of our partnership with God. He's sovereign, yet we are responsible. If at any point He wants to heal someone or save someone or intervene in some way, that is His prerogative as King of the universe. In His kindness, He has also commissioned us—His followers—to form people in His image and to bring about His Kingdom here on earth through a process He gave us called *discipleship*.

It's in this mysterious partnership between the sovereign and the responsible that the "normal" partners with the "miraculous" and disciples of Jesus Christ are made.

- In Matthew 7:24, Jesus says, "Therefore everyone who hears these words of mine and puts them into practice is like a wise man who built his house on the rock."

- In John 3:5–6, Jesus says, "Truly, truly, I say to you, unless one is born of water and the Spirit, he cannot enter the kingdom of God. That which is born of the flesh is flesh, and that which is born of the Spirit is spirit."

- In Matthew 28:18–20, Jesus says, "All authority in heaven and on earth has been given to me. Go therefore and make disciples of all nations, baptizing them in the name of the Father and of the Son and of the Holy Spirit, teaching them to observe all that I have commanded you. And behold, I am with you always, to the end of the age."

- Romans 8:11 says, "If the Spirit of him who raised Jesus from the dead dwells in you, he who raised Christ Jesus from the dead will also give life to your mortal bodies through his Spirit who dwells in you."

- Mathew 19:14 says, "Jesus said, "Let the little children come to me, and do not hinder them, for the kingdom of heaven belongs to such as these."

Child discipleship is where the mundane meets the majestic, and with gold-fish crackers to boot! Sort of like when a child grows an inch—when did that happen? You see it, but you don't see it. How is that?

When we partner with God to reach and disciple children, we do our part to shape children by relying upon the power of God's Word and the work of the Holy Spirit. It's through this partnership that children can respond to the gospel, trust Jesus Christ as their Lord and Savior, and mature in their faith over time. They can grow through Bible teaching and Scripture engagement, through prayer, service, mentorship, conversation, life experiences, and various other discipleship practices (you see it). As children follow Jesus over time (you don't see it), the Holy Spirit transforms them through the ongoing, lifetime process of discipleship to become more like Him.

*It's in this partnership between us (disciple-makers) and God,*
*that the faith of our children is formed.*

Making disciples is the central work of the church. When a church communi-ty homes in on this craft of disciple-making with children, the church is doing the most important work on the planet. This is what parents want and this is what children's ministry leaders in churches want. More than any other research finding, this came across as the singular most unifying goal of those who care about the faith of our children.

## Our Definition of Success

In research project number four, which was conducted in 2019 among chil-dren's ministry leaders in the U.S., we asked the question, "How do you define *success* in children's ministry?" This question was an "open-ended" question, which means the respondents could write in their own top of mind responses. The *5by5 Research Agency* coded the responses (coding is sort of like "tag-ging" in social media based on theme or topic), and the top three responses among the general children's ministry population were:

- Discipleship – 33.2%
- Spiritual Growth – 30.6%
- Salvations – 28.6%[1]

What researchers love about open-ended questions is the "top of mind awareness" factor. That is, open-ended questions can help us extrapolate and understand our initial gut responses as a children's ministry community. Another thing to note here is that respondents were allowed to enter in multiple responses. And these were the top three responses.

The good news here is that our gut response as a community is that we are chiefly concerned about introducing children to Jesus, helping them begin a relationship with Him, growing spiritually, and to begin walking with Jesus as His disciple.

In that same 2019 study, we also asked, "Is the focus of your church's program(s) primarily…"

- Outreach – 1.75%
- Discipleship – 43.2%
- Equally Discipleship and Outreach – 55.1%[2]

What was overwhelmingly clear from this study, is that when it comes to children's ministry, discipleship is the dominant *focus* in our churches and it's how we describe success. When given the opportunity to select "outreach" (proactively reaching kids in the community, evangelism, etc.) as the *singular* focus, fewer than 2 in 100 selected *outreach*. This means that just over 98 percent of U.S. children's ministry leaders view children's ministry as what's called *formational* ministry. Even our selection of "equally discipleship and outreach" says we want to reach out to children to engage them, but with the motivation of not only introducing them to Jesus as their Savior but discipling them as well.

Discipleship is our desired focus and it's how we describe success.

### Reverse Engineering – Start With the End in Mind

In a study Awana commissioned with Barna Research published in 2022 titled *Children's Ministry in a New Reality*, we were trying to understand the desired "outcomes" of children's ministry. In one particular finding below, I grouped the top ten responses under three overarching themes: Relationship with Jesus, Congregational Belonging, and Biblical Understanding. Here's what we were trying to understand:

*Imagine a child who actively engages with everything a ministry offers. When they age out of children's ministry, they should…*

Relationship With Jesus:

- 97% – Know that Jesus loves them
- 86% – Understand their redemption through Jesus Christ
- 83% – Have a personal relationship with Jesus

Congregational Belonging:

- 90% – Feel like a part of the church body
- 87% – Feel comfortable attending the main worship service with adults
- 86% – Feel comfortable joining the church's youth ministry
- 75% – Have a loving, caring relationship with an adult

Biblical Understanding:

- 86% – Understand the big picture of the Bible
- 84% – Know biblical principles
- 76% – Understand the Bible as a unified story[3]

Sort of like reverse engineering, by starting with the desired outcomes of a child "aging out" of a children's ministry, we can see a narrative is emerging, and it's this: When they age out of a children's ministry they should have a relationship with Jesus, and the process to help shape that relationship is through relational belonging and leading children to understand the Bible.

With all you must do each week, it would be easy to set this book down, walk away, move on to your next task and almost forget this. But what if we were to commit this image below to memory? What if we were to view this as an opportunity to reverse engineer our ministry around these insights? Going from right to left, observe the model below:

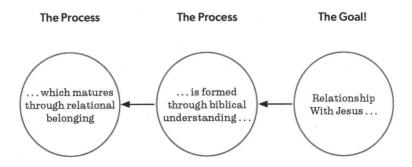

**The Process**          **The Process**          **The Goal!**

...which matures through relational belonging    ←    ...is formed through biblical understanding...    ←    Relationship With Jesus...

Those in the church (pastors, children's ministry leaders, parents, and grandparents) understand that the Bible is not an end unto itself. Rather, when loving, caring adults who exude belonging and care, find ways to engage children in the Bible, the hearts of children can open up to the truth of the Gospel.

So starting with the end in mind, if a relationship with Jesus is the goal, the pathway to help children get there is through a highly relational church community that leads kids to biblical understanding.

### The Discipleship Gap Analysis

Are you familiar with a "gap analysis?" Here's an illustration most of us can relate to—the health of our bodies.

So, let's say you and I are in a health club together. We want to eat well, exercise, cut down on bad habits...all that sort of stuff. At the beginning of our program, our health coach asks us, "On a scale of 1 to 5, with 1 being "not at all important" and 5 being "very important," how important is your overall health?" After discussing this together for a bit, we come up with what we believe is an honest response of 4.7. This is what we'd call our *importance* score. We place an importance on our health of 4.7 out of 5. Now, let's move on from importance to *performance*.

As we get going in our program and start working with our health coach, we begin tracking steps, counting calories, watching what we eat, get the cardio pumping, and all that stuff, then reality begins to emerge. We have good days, and we have bad days, but not only that, we have a final health performance score. Our health coach comes to us and hands us our score of 3.7. What?!? But we worked so hard! This 3.7 score is our *performance* score.

So a gap analysis takes our importance score of 4.7 and compares it to our performance score of 3.7, and as you can see, the difference is –1.0. The *analysis* comes in when we start asking the questions around, "Ok, I worked hard! Why did I only score a 3.7? What can I do to raise my score? How can I close this gap?" This is gap analysis 101.

In a research project we conducted in 2014 with the 5by5 Research Agency, we asked the following question:

> Thinking about the purpose or objective of your church's children's ministry programming, for each of the following statements describing a purpose or objective, first of all tell how important you believe

the purpose/objective is. Please answer using a 5-point scale where 1 is "not important at all" and 5 is "very important."[4]

One of the items we asked respondents to rate was "Producing children who are committed disciples" and the overall importance rating was 4.78.

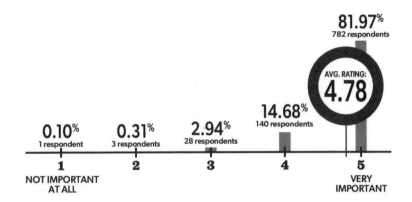

We then asked a follow-up question,

> Next, tell how you believe your church's children's ministry overall is fulfilling each purpose/objective. Please answer using a 5-point scale where 1 is "not fulfilling at all" and 5 is "fulfilling completely."[5]

When it came to our performance, the rating was 3.48. That's a –1.3 gap analysis, which is significant.

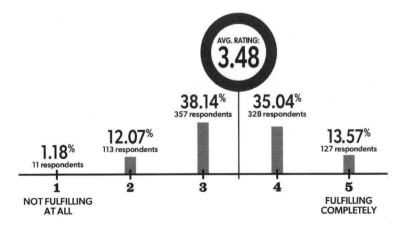

Based on what we've covered thus far in this chapter, it's not surprising that "producing children who are committed disciples" scores so highly in terms of "importance." This is your heartbeat! But when it comes to our performance, we're off the mark. We are under performing our own expectations.

Although we may not be meeting our expectations, and we may not be where we need to be, I'm filled with hope. The reason I'm filled with hope is what we will explore together in chapters two and three. Before we get there, let's close chapter one with a clear definition and a picture of practicality.

## Wait, What Exactly Is Child Discipleship?

Before we go any further, to give us a common framework of thinking, let's define "child discipleship." In 2013, as a global ministry, Awana started asking the question, "What is it the church does that leads to lasting faith in kids?" Now, when we say "church" we mean the church community: pastors, parents, leaders, volunteers, teachers, mentors, etc. As a ministry, we had gained a reputation of helping churches and parents "produce young disciples with lasting faith," but we wanted to know why this was the case. So, we were trying to understand, "What are the primary factors that are most known to shape lasting faith in young people?"

To answer this question, we analyzed the data from the projects we had commissioned alongside research from Barna Group, LifeWay Research, Fuller Youth Institute, Christian Smith, Baylor, and others. In addition, we sifted through the personal letters and testimonies we receive from our missionaries and ministries in over 130 countries around the world—looking for key themes. Last but not least, when we read through the pages of the Gospels we asked ourselves, "When we see Jesus making disciples in the Bible, what do we see Him doing?"

As we evaluated all this data and information, three clear themes began to emerge: Relationships, Scripture engagement, and experiences (or practices).[6] We call these three primary disciple-making factors *Belong, Believe,* and *Become.* In one sentence, our definition of the process of forming a child disciple reads like this:

>  ***Child Discipleship*** is a process designed to form lasting faith
> by helping kids ***belong*** to God and His Kingdom,
> ***believe*** in Jesus Christ as Lord and Savior
> and to ***become*** like Jesus and walk in His ways
> through the power of the Holy Spirit.

*Belong* represents highly relational process that's led by loving, caring adults like parents, church leaders, volunteers, teachers, mentors, and the like. When loving, caring adults exude a highly relational sense of belonging, kids tend to sense love and are more open to the gospel and the Bible. *Believe* is about helping kids discover reality in the truth of the gospel in the Bible. The more a child experiences a culture of rich Scripture engagement, the more likely they are to trust Christ as Savior and grow in their faith. *Become* is the experiential process of helping children and students know how to participate in the world around them. They need loving, caring adults to help them navigate the rapidly changing culture and to experience God through practicing the ways of Jesus.

Your family or church may not use the exact "3B" language we use, but what we have discovered is that the meaning of those three primary factors of relationships, Scripture engagement, and experiences seem to be consistent findings in all of our research. These primary factors seem to be the most fruitful "process" that is used with children to form lasting faith. So, as we move forward together in the pags ahead, we hope this Child Discipleship definition above can give us a common framework of thinking.

### A Practical Picture

As you can likely tell, I'm a visual thinker. I like charts, graphs, and images that can help us grasp concepts to increase insight and learning to lead us to maximum godly wisdom. Before we begin to dive deeper into next level key insights that can shape *how* we form the faith of our children, let's first look at another visual picture that can help frame our thinking about child discipleship most biblically.

The big idea we've covered in this chapter is this: *The single most unifying insight in our research was that the lifelong discipleship of our children is our desired outcome.* Your heartbeat to reach and disciple children came across loud and clear in our research. We heard you and are beyond grateful for the work you do each day to disciple this generation. But what does the child discipleship *journey* (or process) look like?

One of my ministry colleagues, Dr. Ed Gossien, likes to say, "Child discipleship is a lot like boarding a jet. Pre-salvation, the disciple-making process is like walking down the jetway. *Salvation* in Jesus Christ is like stepping over that one-inch gap of faith from the jetway onto the jet. And discipleship continues after salvation. So, the *process* of making a disciple is a pre- and post-salvation journey."

To illustrate, take a look at the three fictional timelines below. Each timeline represents the life and child discipleship journey of a young person who is being formed to trust Christ as Savior and to become like Christ, growing into increased spiritual maturity in young adulthood. Notice that Emily, Griffin, and Olivia each have a unique journey.

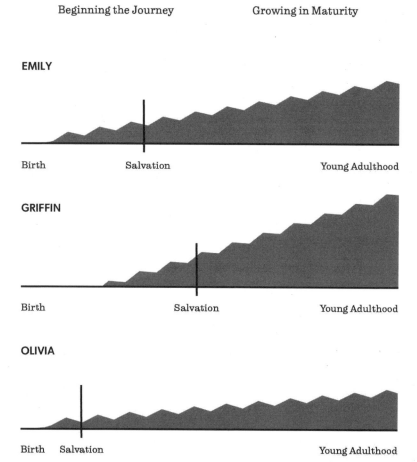

Beginning the Journey      Growing in Maturity

**EMILY**

Birth      Salvation      Young Adulthood

**GRIFFIN**

Birth      Salvation      Young Adulthood

**OLIVIA**

Birth    Salvation      Young Adulthood

What do you notice? We can see that Emily was being shaped (think, "discipleship process") at a very young age to become a disciple but did not trust Christ as her Savior until likely the elementary years when she began to grow as a disciple of Jesus in spiritual maturity. We see that Griffin came to Christ likely in his middle school years and has grown significantly in spiritual maturity as a disciple of Jesus. Then there's Olivia who trusted Christ as Savior at a very young age and has grown quite modestly in spiritual maturity into her young adult years compared to Emily and Griffin.

What Emily, Griffin, and Olivia each share in common is this:

- Child Discipleship was a formational *process* that began prior to salvation by grace through faith in Jesus Christ.

- At various points, each professed faith in Jesus Christ and became a disciple.

- Each one continued to grow in their young adult years at varying levels of spiritual maturity.

- Each one faced spiritual ups and downs in their discipleship journey in the process of growing toward deeper maturity.

You and I never know when a child (or an adult for that matter) is going to trust Christ as his/her Savior. We don't exactly know when a "spiritual growth spurt" is going to take place. Much like when a child grows an inch, we see it, but we don't see it.

What we *do* know is what we discussed earlier in this chapter: Child discipleship is our normal participation with God as He does the work that only He can do through the power of His Word and the work of the Holy Spirit.

*It's in this partnership between us (disciple-makers) and God,*
*that the faith of our children is formed.*

As we move forward into chapters two and three, we will look at what the research says we can do to play our part in forming the faith of our children, while we trust God to do what only He can do.

**Discussion Questions:**

1. Thinking of "forming lasting faith in children," read Revelation 7:9–12. As you imagine being a part of this future, biblical scene, when you look to the right and the left, what faces do you see? Name the people who mean the most to you whom you long to "be there." What children, who are now in your life, do you want to see grow up with a lasting faith to join you and the Kingdom of God in Revelation 7?

2. As discussed in this chapter, at the highest and most conceptual level, child discipleship is a joint effort of us participating with God with the motivation of forming children in the image of God. What are one or two things you do that you think have the most significant impact on

discipling kids? Why do you think that is? What would it look like to do less of the things that have little impact, and more of these things that have the highest impact?

3.  In this chapter, we discussed the 3B definition of what forms a child disciple: Belong (relationships), Believe (Scripture engagement), and Become (experiences). Do these three primary factors resonate with your own personal experience and study? If yes, discuss why? Are there other key factors you think I missed? If so, what are they?

## Endnotes

[1] Research Project Four commissioned by Awana, *5by5 Research Agency* (Nashville, 5by5 Research Agency, 2019), 53.

[2] Research Project Four, 58.

[3] Research Project Seven commissioned by Awana, Barna Group, *Children's Ministry in a New Reality: Building Church Communities That Cultivate Lasting Faith* (Ventura, CA, Barna Group, 2022), 22.

[4] Research Project Two commissioned by Awana, *5by5 Research Agency* (Nashville, 5by5 Research Agency, 2014), 3.

[5] Research Project Two, 5.

[6] Valerie Bell, Matt Markins, and Mike Handler, *Resilient: Child Discipleship and the Fearless Future of the Church* (St. Charles, IL, Awana, 2020), 170–171.

CHAPTER 2

# RELATIONSHIPS

## The Most Catalytic Factor in
## Forming Lasting Faith in Children

**The single most catalytic factor to influence the formation of lasting faith in children is loving, caring, adult relationships.**

If I were to ask you, who was the *one person* in your life that made a significant spiritual impact in your discipleship journey, who would you say? Was it a teacher, coach, children's church leader, a parent, or grandparent? And what life phase were you in: childhood, middle school, high school, young adult, or adult?

When I ask the question in a live setting at a workshop, hands go up across the room as quickly as the names are shouted out loud: Jeff, Emma, Brandi, Patty, Mike, Sarah, my mom...and the names keep coming. As I dig a little deeper and ask, "Can you tell me the story?" it's often followed by tears. I often hear,

- "My dad was never around, so Jose stepped in and took me to baseball practice..."
- "Shelly would meet me in the park, take me out for ice cream, and go on walks with me..."
- "Every morning when I would wake up, my mom was in the dimly lit kitchen reading her Bible and praying..."
- "Jerome was not only my sixth-grade teacher, but my small group leader and mentor..."
- "Dad was the best man I'd ever known. He was quiet, but when he spoke to me, it was meaningful and powerful..."

And the tears just flow.

Why is this? Why is it these people mean so much to us? And why do we have such a fondness and affection in our hearts for them? To understand this phenomenon most fully, we must go back to eternity past.

In eternity past, God was fully content and delighted in the fellowship of the three persons of the Trinity: God the Father, God the Son, and God the Holy Spirit. In God's perfection, there is unity, love, and relational harmony in the three persons of the Trinity. We hear delight and anticipation in our Creator's voice when He says, "Let us make man in our image, after our likeness" in Genesis 1:26. In God's generosity, He created us to be in relationship and fellowship with Him. What a gift! As if that wasn't enough, He gave Adam another human, Eve, and told them to be fruitful and multiply and to fill the earth and subdue it to perpetuate the community building.

So why do we tear up when we describe how much these loving, caring adults mean to us?

We are *Imago Dei*. Created in the image of God. Just as God experiences pure delight in perfect fellowship within the three persons of the Trinity, in a similar (but imperfect) way we can also experience loving relationships with the people God has placed in our lives. When it comes to forming children as His disciples, it's this one, single factor, that shows up as being the most *catalytic* when it comes to forming the faith of our children.

In the context of a church community, through relationships, a child can get access to:

- Love, care, and safety
- Having their most basic needs met
- Someone who can walk with them through traumatic experiences
- Additional educational opportunities
- Hear and respond to the gospel
- Learn about Jesus through the Bible
- Formation as a young, growing disciple

Simply put, *relationship* is the currency of the Kingdom of Heaven. It's what He gave us in the Garden of Eden. It's what we regain through the work of Jesus Christ. It's what we possess in the power of the Holy Spirit. Therefore, it should be no surprise to us that when it comes to forming the faith of our children, the most *catalytic* factor to form their faith is relationship.

As a disciple of Jesus Christ, we are on a pilgrimage *to* God. We are not walking through this earth aimlessly, we are walking with Him and to Him in our quite imperfect state, but one day, we will be fully restored and united with Him in Heaven.

It's what He gave us in the Garden of Eden. It's what we regain through the work of Jesus Christ. It's what we possess in the power of the Holy Spirit. Therefore, it should be no surprise to us that when it comes to forming the faith of our children, the most *catalytic* factor to form their faith is relationship.

## The Catalytic Factor – Loving, Caring, Adult Relationships

First things first, what is a *catalyst*? A catalyst is a person, thing, or an event that causes change or some sort of action.

In descriptive language, a catalyst is like a spark that gets a fire going. At one point, we have dry tender (wood) but no fire, then there's a spark, followed by a fire. How did we go from no fire...to a fire? The spark changed the conditions of the environment. The friction between the flint and the steel created a spark that ignited the dry tender and then, poof! I. Have. Made. Fire!

Over the past decade, when we've (Awana) studied the faith formation of our children, we see a similar pattern as the "dry tender → spark → fire" pattern. To be explicitly clear, and oversimplified, it can look like this:

- A child has little-to-no relationship with God →
- A loving, caring, adult disciple-maker enters the life of a child →
- A child is now given the opportunity to →
    - Hear and respond to the gospel
    - Be taught the Bible
    - Learn about Jesus
    - Practice the way of Jesus
    - Enjoy a place of belonging
    - Engage in service and ministry
    - Grow in faith and maturity

As we've studied and asked, "What was the factor that sparked a child's faith to go from little-to-no relationship with God, to a growing relationship with God?" the clear, primary factor is the relationship with at least one loving, caring, adult disciple-maker. That observation was especially clear in our 2022 research project with Barna Group.

In our eighth research project, published in 2022, Barna Group discovered that, "Today, two in five churched parents of 5–14-year-olds (39%) indicate their child has a meaningful relationship with an adult at their church. Specifically, these adults say their child has a positive, meaningful relationship with another adult at church and also say it's "completely true" their child has a meaningful relationship with a mentoring adult through their church."[3]

## Two in Five Children in Children's Ministry Have a Meaningful Relationship With an Adult

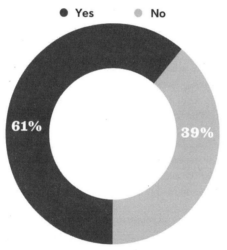

n=1,021 U.S. churched adults with a child ages 5–14 at home, June 11–July 6, 2021.

So the good news is that nearly 40 percent of children attending church in the U.S. have a meaningful relationship with an adult at church. On the downside, this could be so much stronger. What if this were 50 percent or even 60 percent? How different would our culture look?

The real story, though, is in the next two charts. Be sure to notice that the dark gray bars are children who have a meaningful adult relationship at church and the light gray bars are children who do not have a meaningful adult relationship at church. What do you see?

## Parents of 5–14 year-olds: Thinking about your child and their experience at church, how true are the following about them?[2]

*"My child …" % say "completely true"*

● Child has a meaningful adult relationship
● Child does not have a meaningful adult relationship

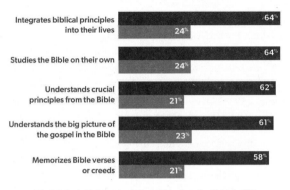

| | |
|---|---|
| Integrates biblical principles into their lives | 64% / 24% |
| Studies the Bible on their own | 64% / 24% |
| Understands crucial principles from the Bible | 62% / 21% |
| Understands the big picture of the gospel in the Bible | 61% / 23% |
| Memorizes Bible verses or creeds | 58% / 21% |

n=1,021 U.S. churched adults with a child ages 5–14 at home, June 11–July 6, 2021.

## Parents of 5–14-year-olds: "At church, my child has the opportunity to . . ."[3]

*% "completely true"*

● Child has a meaningful adult relationship
● Child does not have a meaningful adult relationship

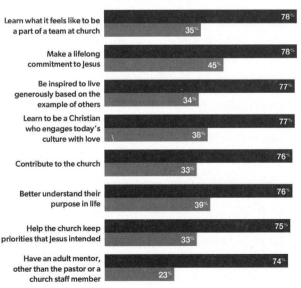

| | |
|---|---|
| Learn what it feels like to be a part of a team at church | 78% / 35% |
| Make a lifelong commitment to Jesus | 78% / 45% |
| Be inspired to live generously based on the example of others | 77% / 34% |
| Learn to be a Christian who engages today's culture with love | 77% / 38% |
| Contribute to the church | 76% / 33% |
| Better understand their purpose in life | 76% / 39% |
| Help the church keep priorities that Jesus intended | 75% / 33% |
| Have an adult mentor, other than the pastor or a church staff member | 74% / 23% |

It's not even close.

When children are in a church community where they have access to a meaningful relationship with a loving, caring adult, we often see children engaging more in the practices of the faith.

One thing to note here, is that these loving, caring adults can be a parent, a volunteer, a kids' pastor, a small group leader, a mentor, or a grandparent. Ideally, a Christian young person would grow up in a home with a mother and a father who are both actively discipling their children. Unfortunately, this is not the reality for most children. Whether a child is growing in a single-parent home or in a two-partent home, discipleship is simply not taking place. This is precisely why this research is so important.

The power behind the "one loving, caring adult" research is about forming *spiritual resiliency* in children...kids who will grow in their faith despite less-than-ideal circumstances. The message to us is this:

> Ideally (and biblically), the children in our church would have a home where they are being discipled by their parents. But even if it's not taking place at home, the church can still be a place of significant impact. We should strive to equip and empower parents to disciple their own children. Yet, there is hope for the kids who are not being discipled at home.

> Church leaders must equip the saints to disciple their own kids, *and* equip the saints to disciple the children God brings to our church.

This same idea showed up in an Awana impact study conducted by Excellence in Giving in 2020 where we surveyed almost 1,100 past participants. We learned that "Awana became the #1 factor in the formation of faith for children who did not have a good relationship with mom or dad at home."[4] For children who do have healthy relationships at home, parents tend to be more influential on the spiritual formation of their children, but not all children are so blessed to live in a home with healthy relational dynamics. This is where the church comes in to play. By having experiences like Awana, a small group, or a discipleship group, kids can get access to a meaningful adult relationship.

Just one, loving, caring, adult disciple-maker can be the catalyst to form lasting faith in children.

> Church leaders: we must craft a culture where kids belong. A highly relational culture where children are named, seen, valued, engaged, have a voice, are known, and feel a sense of belonging. When we do

this, kids are far more likely to "hear and see" the gospel, listen to the Bible being taught, and take steps forward in their faith.

Parents and Caregivers: we must put the phone down. We need to remove distractions and engage with our children relationally. Let's get to know our children, observe their uniqueness, name their strengths and God-given talents, and speak blessing over their lives. Pray over them. Introduce them to Jesus, engage them in the Bible, and share our faith stories with them.

Overall, how are we doing at this? Let's look at the child disciple-maker "relationship" gap analysis.

### The Child Disciple-Maker "Relationship" Gap Analysis

In chapter one, we discussed the gap analysis (remember our health coach?). Thinking about importance vs. performance, we also asked in that same study,

> Thinking about the purpose or objective of your church's children's ministry programming, for each of the following statements describing a purpose or objective, first of all tell how important you believe the purpose/objective is. Please answer using a 5-point scale where 1 is "not important at all" and 5 is "very important."[5]

> Developing discipleship relationships between children's ministry workers and the children they serve.

> Importance – 4.54

Relating to our performance, we then asked,

> Next, tell how you believe your church's children's ministry overall is fulfilling each purpose/objective. Please answer using a 5-point scale where 1 is "not fulfilling at all" and 5 is "fulfilling completely."[6]

> Developing discipleship relationships between children's ministry workers and the children they serve.

> Performance – 3.52

It's no surprise that children's ministry leaders rated the importance of "Developing discipleship relationships between children's ministry workers and the children they serve" so highly. We should find this aspiration rather encouraging! Yet, as of the time of this study, we're experiencing a gap of –1.2

in our performance. Making sure kids have safe and loving adult relationships is important to us, but we're not quite where we'd like to be.

So, what does this –1.2 gap in our performance actually mean? Think of it this way, if you were up for a performance review at work and you rated your own performance a 4.54 and your boss rated you a 3.52, your boss's evaluation of your performance is off by over 20 percent from your self-evaluation. This would create some interesting discussion between you and your boss. In focus groups we commissioned in 2019 with children's ministry leaders, here's just a few of the qualitative comments recorded:

- "You can have the best curriculum in the world, but if you don't have the best leaders [to teach or facilitate], it doesn't matter."
- "We can't keep up with the growth. We have more kids than we have [volunteers]. Our engagement level stays at the surface because we are just trying to survive."
- "I have difficulty gaining enough volunteers to keep children's ministry running. Parents like the ministry but are engaged in their own small group or Sunday School class."
- "It's important that our volunteers are inspired and equipped. Investing in our volunteers is a huge priority to me...a lot of my time goes into recruiting and working with our volunteers."[7]

Do you, too, feel this *gap* of not having enough loving, caring adults to help disciple the children in your ministry?

## Falling Short in Our Area of Greatest Need

In this same study as the qualitative comments directly before this, we asked,

What is your greatest need/where do you need help to make your children's ministry as successful and impactful as possible?[8]

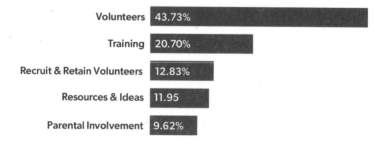

First, it's important to note that this was an open-ended question (these are top of mind responses, not selections from a checklist). Second, these were the top five responses. Lastly, it's also worth noting that out of these responses, four out of the five are *relational*. "Resources & ideas" is the only area not explicitly connected to volunteers, training or recruiting volunteers, or parental involvement.

We know this. As children's ministry leaders, we live with a keen sense of awareness that our deepest needs are relational needs. Ideas and resources are important...creativity and planning are foundational, but these are not the *catalytic* drivers. What we are looking for are loving, caring adults (child disciple-makers) who want to come along on this journey with us. Not just any journey. The most important trek on the planet as we disciple a generation who will experience a future world we can hardly imagine.

That anxiety you carry in your gut and the weight you heap over your shoulder is that –1.2 gap. A –1.2 gap may not seem overwhelming on paper, but it shows up in the way your body is carrying that stress. It shows up in sleepless nights, a feeling of isolation during staff meetings, and resignation fraught Monday's.

It's clear from Scriptures, it's clear from our intuitive experience, and it even shows up in the research: The single most *catalytic* factor to influence the formation of lasting faith in children is loving, caring, adult relationships.

Yet, we live in a world of the –1.2 gap where the harvest is plentiful, and the laborers are few.

### We Must Change Our Mindset – The Faith-Filled Mystery of Gideon's Army

Can you imagine how Gideon (Judges 7) must have felt? I mean, he's staring down the Midianite army and only has 32,000 men—and God brings Gideon's army down to 10,000 men. Then He announces He's not through yet and puts a process to bring Gideon's army down to only 300 men! If I was Gideon, in my flesh, I would have been so tempted to exclaim, "Seriously God? Look at what you are asking of me, and instead of giving me more soldiers, you are taking away soldiers!?!" Oh me of little faith.

Thinking back to our gap analysis, Gideon was facing a bit of a gap himself. He starts out with 32,000 men (when he probably would have liked to have had far more, just to be safe) and he ends up with only 300 men. That's a gap of –31,700 soldiers. That's no small gap!

Yet, it's in our gaps when God does His best work.

In the gap, we feel vulnerable, weak, exposed, and powerless. Because we are.

When we look in the Scriptures, we see humanity's vulnerable gap:

- God rescued Noah and his family in an ark
- God provided a substitute for Abraham and Isaac
- God parted the waters for His oppressed and trapped people
- Jesus wrapped Himself in our flesh and took up the pain of our humanity
- Jesus calmed the storms and along with it the fears of men
- Jesus miraculously multiped bread and fed hungry stomachs

As North Americans, we've become so dependent upon our human systems, that when we face gaps, we tend to fill that gap with a sense of failure or rejection. According to the Scriptures, we need to turn away from this thinking and when we face these gaps (like Gideon) turn our dependence back to the God of the mustard seed.

> What if, instead of filling that gap (not enough loving, caring adults) with shame, we stuff it with gratitude for what God is going to do?

> Instead of placing the worry and anxiety in the gap, we fill it with prayers of faith.

> Instead of filling the gap with fear and rejection, let's replace it with joy and gratitude.

> Let's fill the gap with vision casting and personal invitations for those God wants to invite along on this important journey—no matter how few or many that may be (think "Gideon's army"). Then trust God to do the rest.

The single most catalytic factor to influence the formation of lasting faith in children is relationships—the currency of the Kingdom of Heaven. Yet, we never seem to have enough adults willing to engage, teach, facilitate, lead, and love children.

When Gideon lost 31,700 of his army, this gap created his weakest and most vulnerable moment and that's when God did the work that only He could do. God did it His way, and Gideon's army was victorious. Let's stuff our gap (not enough loving, caring, adult child disciple-makers...not enough parents stepping up) with joyful anticipation, worship of a creative God, gratitude for what He's going to do, and trust for His future generosity. Then, let's watch God solve our gaps in ways that cause us to say, "Wow. Only the God of the mustard seed."

So, where do we go from here? The chapters ahead will shed additional light on a recommended pathway forward. Let's keep going.

**Discussion Questions:**

1.  When you think about your own discipleship journey, was there a key person who was catalytic to your spiritual journey?

2.  With the kids in your personal life (children, grandchildren, nieces, nephews, kids you mentor, etc.), how would you rate your relational connection with them? Do these kids feel a sense of belonging with you? Do they know they can talk with you about anything and that you will love them unconditionally?

3.  Would you say your church community is highly relational with children? Is your church a place where kids feel seen, known, and have a feeling of belonging?

4.  If a church community were Scripture rich and really good at Bible teaching, but not so good at making kids feel a sense of relational belonging, what do you think would be the potential down-side of that church community?

5.  As a parent or a child-influencer, what one thing can you do to become more fruitful at relational connection with kids for the sake of the gospel? As a church leader or church volunteer, what one thing can you do to become more fruitful at relational connection with kids for the sake of the gospel?

## Endnotes

[1] Research Project Seven, 72.

[2] Research Project Seven, 74.

[3] Research Project Seven, 77.

[4] Research Project Six commissioned by *Awana, Excellence in Giving, Awana U.S. Impact Study* (Colorado Springs, CO, EIG, 2020), 6.

[5] Research Project Two, 3.

[6] Research Project Two, 5.

[7] Research Project Four, 40–42.

[8] Research Project Four, 86.

# CHAPTER 3

# BIBLE ENGAGEMENT

## The Most Foundational Factor in Forming Lasting Faith in Children

**The most foundational factor to influence the formation of lasting faith in children is Bible engagement.**

Check out these headlines from just the past few years on Bible engagement:

> *Teens Hold High View of the Bible but Don't Read It Often, Barna Finds* (Baptist Press)
>
> *Fewer in U.S. Now See the Bible as Literal Word of God* (Gallup News)
>
> *Nearly 40% of Gen Z Adults Believe Jesus Wasn't Sinless: Survey* (Christian Post)
>
> *Unprecedented Drop in Bible Engagement Among U.S. Adults (Good-FaithMedia.org)*

With just some basic internet searches, you can find these articles and a whole lot more.

Now, let's correlate these types of headlines alongside of the 2019 publishing of *Faith for Exiles* by David Kinnaman and Mark Matlock. In *Faith for Exiles*, Kinnaman and Matlock say that only ten percent of the 18- to 29-year-olds in the U.S. who follow Jesus are what they call "resilient disciples."[1] These resilient disciples experience Jesus personally, display cultural discernment, have meaningful Christian relationships, and they live out countercultural mission and vocational discipleship. Their counterparts, however, have left the church (22%), are unchurched (30%), and are habitual churchgoers who are not intentional, engaged disciples (38%).[2]

Collectively—the church at large in the U.S.—our success rate at forming resilient disciples (young people who thrive in their faith in the midst of a secular age) is ten percent. Sort of like when you are watching the big game in your living room and your friend walks in during the third quarter and says, "What's the score? How are we doing?" In a similar vein, how are we doing? One in ten. What is our score, our outcome, our success rate? Ten percent.

I'd like to argue that there is a *correlative* connection between the drop in Bible engagement over the last few decades and our output of ten percent resilient disciples among emerging young adults. Now, for something to be *causal* you must show the direct cause of one factor impacting another. I'm not making a *causal* argument, but I am arguing that these two factors are *correlative*, meaning there is a corresponding relationship between the drop in Bible engagement and our output of resilient disciples. There's a connection...a mutual relationship. And I think we can see where it's been happening specifically in children's ministry in the U.S.

If you go back to the 1980s, 1990s and early 2000s, while the public school system and the world of entertainment was moving at full speed toward Darwinian naturalism, the church in the U.S. was simultaneously moving toward a popular-level, Bible Lite Strategy.[3] Naturalism tells a compelling philosophical and scientific story that all the properties of the universe came about as a result of natural processes. Not only is this story devoid of the divine, but as it's been told in recent decades, it's also packaged with a romanticized view of self that's been fueled by the emerging technological innovations that supposedly can help us progress toward the secular utopia. Every bit of this has been in lockstep with the "science is what's real" message from the scientific community. This progressive march toward the secular utopia has been entirely aimed at the most formative among us—our children. If, for some reason, this wasn't clear in past decades, it's become crystal clear over the past ten years.

Simultaneously, instead of matching this compelling, progressive, secular utopian story with the robust power of the fullness of the gospel story arc (Creation, Fall, redemption, restoration) from the Bible, much of the church in the U.S. met the moment with the popularized Bible Lite Strategy. The Bible Lite Strategy manifests itself as moralism or legalism on the right and Moralistic Therapeutic Deism on the left.[4] So what has this looked like? Over the past few decades, the church in the U.S. put a tremendous amount of effort into teaching the Bible as a set of values, virtues, and moralistic stories, but without the core infrastructure of a central spine (the gospel arc found in the Bible) that a child can attach them to in order to build a Christ-centered worldview. So let's define what's happening here:

The **Bible Lite Strategy** emphasizes values, virtues, morals, or character from the Bible in a way that's unrooted from the gospel. It isn't always inaccurate, but it is incomplete. Good character is not the goal of a Christian; it's the byproduct of a life surrendered to and cultivated in Jesus Christ.[5]

Naturalism has been a dominant cultural narrative over the past 50 years, and it tells a child, "You came about because of natural processes. There is no master designer. There is no universal truth. You are free to make up your own meaning and purpose." So, when a church teaches values and virtues in the secular, post-Christian culture we now live in, and we don't give children the clear, compelling, narrative of the gospel, a child is going to take that virtue (let's say "kindness") and attach that virtue to the narrative that they do know and experience in their everyday life. The dominant narratives that today's kids know are not only naturalism, but also hedonism, and Moralistic Therapeutic Deism (which is essentially the religion of the air). Simply put, the Bible Lite Strategy in its incompleteness ends up fueling the secular, cultural narratives because it gives children the virtues in the absence of careful, nuanced gospel context. Therefore, the child ends up trying to make sense of the virtue (e.g., kindness) in the midst of a cultural narrative that says, "It's *unkind* not to approve of my beliefs or behavior" (whatever those beliefs or behavior may be). In the absence of a clearly articulated gospel narrative, these subtle nuances in our messaging and communication to children become significant.

Christian virtues are essential. Christlike character and values are the fruit of a child's life cultivated in Jesus. But virtues fit within a superstructure (spine or framework) or worldview. For the Christian, that framework or worldview is the gospel. The gospel gives a child the narrative structure of:

- **Creation** – I was made, I know who made me, and I have value and purpose
- **Fall** – I know where sin comes from, I know what's wrong with me, and I know what's wrong with the world
- **Redemption** – I know who paid for my sin, who can save me from my sin, and ultimately save me from the penalty of death, and
- **Restoration** – I know who can lead me to abundant life. I know who can change and transform me, and I know one day all will be renewed to a perfect state in Heaven.

Our children are drowning in powerful secular, cultural narratives that have formed a storytelling superstructure that's all about hyper-individualism. Me.

Me. Me. As we can tell from the isolation and anxiety epidemics, it's failing them. Not only that, the Bible Lite Strategy that many churches in the U.S. have used to meet this cultural moment is also failing our children by giving them moralism, when what kids really need is the gospel. Today's children need to be engaged in environments that are saturated with the Bible...God's Word. As we give them God's Word, we must help them understand not only things like virtues and behaviors, but also the "why" underneath. Nothing does this better than giving them the gospel story arch—nothing is more satisfying than God's story of reality (Creation, Fall, redemption, restoration). Why? Because it's what's real...and every other competing narrative is a lie.

Over the last decade, as we've commissioned numerous research projects, this finding has been overwhelmingly clear: The most foundational factor to influence the formation of lasting faith in children is Bible engagement. Let's dig into the key findings.

## Let's Start With Curriculum

As the saying goes, "Where two or three children's ministry leaders are gathered, they are going to discuss curriculum." Is that a saying? I don't know, but I know it's often true. We hear things like this everywhere we go, right? "I know you guys used to use _____ curriculum? Are you still using that, or did you decide to write your own?" These are typical discussions in the "church world."

Not only are they typical, but I dare say important! What you teach your children each week is essential to your mission of reaching kids with the gospel and engaging them in ongoing discipleship. You are careful and intentional about selecting a curriculum, and for that we all say, "Thank you!"

In a 2013 study Awana conducted, we were trying to identify the primary factors a children's ministry leader considers when selecting a curriculum. We asked this open-ended question,

> What would you say is the single most important
> decision-making factor when you are considering using
> a children's program or materials for your church?[6]

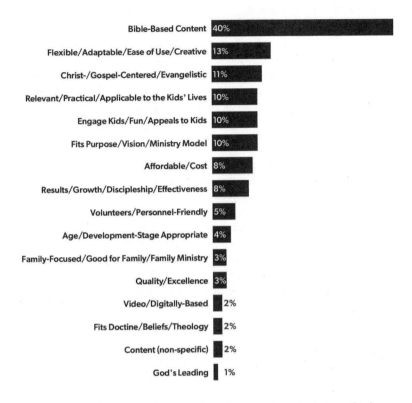

| | |
|---|---|
| Bible-Based Content | 40% |
| Flexible/Adaptable/Ease of Use/Creative | 13% |
| Christ-/Gospel-Centered/Evangelistic | 11% |
| Relevant/Practical/Applicable to the Kids' Lives | 10% |
| Engage Kids/Fun/Appeals to Kids | 10% |
| Fits Purpose/Vision/Ministry Model | 10% |
| Affordable/Cost | 8% |
| Results/Growth/Discipleship/Effectiveness | 8% |
| Volunteers/Personnel-Friendly | 5% |
| Age/Development-Stage Appropriate | 4% |
| Family-Focused/Good for Family/Family Ministry | 3% |
| Quality/Excellence | 3% |
| Video/Digitally-Based | 2% |
| Fits Doctrine/Beliefs/Theology | 2% |
| Content (non-specific) | 2% |
| God's Leading | 1% |

I love open-ended questions because they give us a view at what we think at a gut-level. What's your gut response? Your intuitive sense? This is why open-ended research questions help us move toward understanding.

What encourages me here is that the leading response was "Bible-Based Content." Right at 40 percent of the respondents willingly offered that this is an important factor when considering a children's ministry program. Knowing that Christians are "people of the book," I'm not surprised that "Bible" was the leading response, but it does make me wonder, why wasn't this considered a leading factor for 50 percent, 70 percent, or even 90 percent of respondents? As Christ-followers who are to feast upon the words of God, this does give us a lot to ponder.

Further, when we look at the second, fourth, and fifth place selections, we see items like flexibility, ease of use, relevance, fun, appealing to kids, etc. If I were a kid's pastor, I'd want to spend a lot more time with my team discussing, "Exactly how important are these factors? What role do they play within our ministry?" Clearly, no one wants a curriculum or a program that's clunky, difficult, or complicated. Neither do we want children to be bored. Jesus was anything but boring. The discussion I'd want to have with my team is understanding how much of a grip these American/Western values have on our starting assumptions—and how might these starting assumptions be impacting our effectiveness in the highly secular world we live in. We placed high value on "fun" and "relevance" in past decades, but what role will those factors play as we move into 2030, 2035, and beyond?

What do I mean by this? Let's keep digging.

If you keep looking down the chart in the eighth place you will find "Results/ Growth/Discipleship/Effectiveness." The more we (parents, pastors, children's ministry leaders, etc.) deepen our understanding of the impact that secularism, naturalism, and post-Christian culture is having on the life formation of our children, the more we will keep asking harder questions about the correlation between (1) what we are doing in our children's ministries and (2) the "results" or "effectiveness" of the discipleship of our children. This survey was conducted in 2013. I suspect if this survey were given today, we might see this same item a bit higher, but as we move into the next decade, we can likely expect this idea of "results or effectives" to become even more and more of a conversation.

Let me make one more observation before we leave this 2013 study. I think there is a three-way correlation between the following three data points:

- Bible-Based Content – 40%
- Christ-/Gospel-Centric/Evangelic – 11%
- Results/Growth/Discipleship/Effectiveness – 8%

If we were to reverse-engineer these three data points in one sentence, it would go something like this:

> If we want to increase our effectiveness at discipling children with faith that lasts, we must teach our children the Bible in a way that's Christ-centric and makes the Gospel story arch crystal clear, as we saturate our kids' lives in Bible-rich environments.

The lasting faith of our children is what we long for. It's what makes our heart pump a little faster. If we want lasting faith in our children, we've got to dig that foundation even deeper. When we do, we fill it with not only a Scripture-rich environment where kids' lives are saturated with the Bible, but we also give kids the gospel worldview...a worldview that's far more satisfying than the empty promises of hyper individualism.

**The Bible Engagement Gap Analysis**

In the same 2013 study above, we also asked the same basic question as above, but we gave children's ministry leaders a list of options to choose from giving them a 1–5 point scale where 1 is "not important at all" and 5 is "very important." I was encouraged that the top two selections were "Bible teaching as a part of the program" (4.92) and "Gospel-centered teaching and lessons" (4.78).[7] As a community, we selected these two options above pragmatism, above cost, above number of volunteers, and beyond.

Parents, grandparents, pastors, mentors, and children's ministry leaders, we are people of the Bible. We know the Bible is God's inspired, true, authoritative, and reliable Word. His thoughtful message to humanity. I'm encouraged to know that when it comes to the faith formation of our children, we select the "Bible" and "Gospel-centered teaching" as the most foundational aspects of our children's ministry.

So how are we doing? What's our performance? Thinking about importance vs. performance, in our 2014 study, we asked,

> Thinking about the purpose or objective of your church's children's ministry programming, for each of the following statements describing a purpose or objective, first of all tell how important you believe the purpose/objective is. Please answer using a 5-point scale where 1 is "not important at all" and 5 is "very important."[8]

> Helping children develop a love for studying and knowing the Bible

> Importance – 4.81

In this gap analysis study, helping children know the Bible ranked as the highest aspiration out of all our hopes, dreams, prayers, and goals. It ranked above relationships, it scored higher than missions...it even ranked higher than discipleship itself! When it comes to the Bible, as a community we believe helping kids to know how to engage it is of utmost importance.

Then relating to our performance, we asked,

> Next, tell how you believe your church's children's ministry overall is fulfilling each purpose/objective. Please answer using a 5-point scale where 1 is "not fulfilling at all" and 5 is "fulfilling completely."[9]

> Helping children develop a love for studying and knowing the Bible

> Performance – 3.64

Remembering that these are self-reported responses from the children's ministry community, as a group we're saying we have a gap of –1.17. Of all the "gaps" we identified in this study, this one is not the largest, it's not the smallest, and neither are we overperforming. But it is a gap. So, how are we doing? What does this mean?

Having studied not only this item, but this item in context to each of the others, I think the message is this. We're doing okay. Not great, but not poor either. Our gap here is not near as large as our gaps relating to cultural formation or parent engagement (which we will cover in upcoming chapters). Yet, we are still not meeting our own expectations.

Having read all the "qualitative" responses in these same studies, the message here is that we are seeing some fruit in this area. We *do* see kids in our ministry who are developing a love for God's Word. We are seeing movement. We are seeing the Holy Spirit grab ahold of children and lead them into relationship with God and as a part of that journey, the Bible is playing a key role in the process.

Here's another reason why I say this. In this same gap analysis, we rated the importance of Scripture memory as 4.29 and we scored the performance as 3.58 for a gap of –0.71.[10] Of all the gaps, this was one of the lower gaps. Again, this score/metric also fits the qualitative responses that we do see fruit that leading children to engage the Bible is not only foundational, but that it's fruitful. Yet, we want to see more fruitful results. The score of "we're doing okay" is good, but not good enough. We long to see children who love Jesus and who understand that a key part of how kids walk in relationship with Jesus is to engage His Word as they grow and develop.

## Bible as the Source of Reality

Every child is asking a question. Well, not just "a" question, but a series of inescapable and systemic questions (*Imago Dei*). One of those questions is "What's real?" As kids grow, they want to know, "Of all the competing messages coming my direction, which ones should I be listening to? Which ones can I rely on? Which ones can I build my life upon?"

I love the way Jesus communicates in Matthew 5:27–28 when He says, "You have heard that it was said.... But I tell you...." To paraphrase the meaning, Jesus is essentially saying, "The culture is telling you this.... But I'm about to tell you what's real...." A bit further down in the Gospel of Matthew we find Jesus wrapping up His manifesto to living out the Kingdom of Heaven in Chapter 7.

If we reverse engineer Jesus' words (paraphrasing again) in Matthew 7:24–27, His message is this:

- You want a life that's secure, solid, and good?
- Put into practice...
- ...these words you've just heard me say (in Matthew 5–7).

As we think about Jesus' brilliant communication style when He says, "You've heard it said...," consider these messages the dominant cultures are sending our children 24/7. These messages go a little something like this:

- Hi, I'm digital capitalism. I'm going to show you happiness. If you just keep spending and purchasing these items, you'll have it baby! Oh, look over here! Did you see this one? Ohhh. Must have this one, too!
- Heeey! I'm hedonism. Feeling good?! No? Oh, you're bored, eh? Why be bored...there's a whole world of pleasures over here that's sure to make you feel happy. There's this one, and that one, and oh my look over here!
- Yo, what's up! I'm post-Christendom. I'm "the now." So, what do you have to offer me? Hmm, let's see here. Ok, I'll take love, I'll take joy and freedom and peace and justice. And I want restoration and I'll even take a little kindness and goodness. But! But, but, but, I don't want the *source* from which they come from. Nope. Don't want the Bible, certainly don't want the church, and when it comes to Jesus, I'll take the kind stuff, but His thoughts on sexuality are just *way, way* too restrictive.
- What's up my friend! I'm the sexual revolution. Yesterday you may have known me as one thing, but today I'm something new! And tomorrow? Who knows! Some people say I contradict myself, but I say to that, no! Or yes! Or, whatever, who cares...let's see what happens next!
- Hello there! I'm Moralistic Therapeutic Deism. Yes, I know, my parents cursed me with a dreadfully long name. Here's what I'm gonna do for you. We're gonna take a little bit of this "God and Jesus stuff" and just mix it in with the rest of the cultural salad, and let's call it a deal. Wadda ya say?
- Good evening. I'm honored to meet you. I'm science. I'm sure you've heard about me, because, of course, well, I'm what's real. I'm also the authority. If I say it, you must believe it. Hehe.

What do each of these worldviews and narratives have in common? Two words: Hyper individualization. One word: Self.

What's more? The cultural infrastructure that today's child is swimming in is designed to pump the "hyper individualization steroids" into the blood stream. The screens infrastructure of social media ecosystems like TikTok, Instagram, YouTube, and the unkept playground of the Internet are designed to fuel this self-obsession narrative.

Then there's Jesus. Jesus is saying, "You have heard that it was said...."

Don't you just wonder, if Jesus could have a direct talk with "today's child" what exactly would He say? For those of us who work with kids, we know that "imagination" is a big part of childhood. So, let's use our imaginations for a moment. What do you think He would say to today's child who is swimming in all these secular messages? I think He would say something like,

> My child, you've been told all these other ways will fulfill you. I can tell you are looking for the good life. But I tell you, I _am_ life. I'm actually the source of it! You want the good life? I have abundant life to offer you. I am exactly what you are looking for. Come be with Me. Come and follow Me.

Today's child isn't starting from a "blank cultural slate." Today's child is hearing the Bible being taught in the context of these dominant cultural narratives. This is just one more reason why the Bible Lite Strategy is powerless in standing up against the unending cultural waves. Think about this approach to teaching the virtue of "love." If the virtue of the month is "love your neighbor" and we drop that virtue into the context of today's dominant cultural narratives of "Love is affirming of my lifestyle" (whatever that lifestyle may be), this approach to teaching children the Bible is insufficient and unclear at best and deceptive at worst.

Our children need to know what's real. They need a framework for reality. Where did I come from? Where did all of this come from? Why is something "off" with the world? Why do I sometimes think bad thoughts and do bad things? Yet, why do I also think and do good things?! Who can help me?

In our 2022 study with Barna Group, _Children's Ministry in a New Reality_, we asked children's ministry leaders: "In your children's ministry, how often do you do any of the following?" We listed 11 possible common activities that take place within a children's ministry.[11] First and foremost, and once again, I was deeply encouraged to see the leading response was:

## Study the Bible

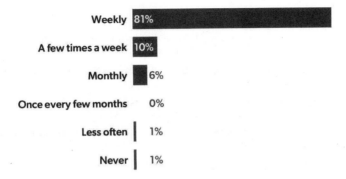

Thankfully, 91 percent of our children's ministries are helping children study the Bible weekly or a few times a week. Praise be to God! Yet...I think we have a big opportunity to increase our child discipleship fruitfulness. Check this out. Near the bottom of that same list (10th out of 11) was the following:

## Learn about a biblical worldview

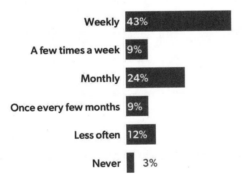

There's another important correlation here, and we have an opportunity to change our perspective and increase our discipleship effectiveness. Here it is:

Helping children have a biblical worldview isn't a
"separate activity" from Bible teaching, it's a key way
that we lead children to understand and engage the Bible.

Sadly, we can use the Bible Lite Strategy and teach kids about all sorts of values and virtues like love, joy, empathy, peace, patience, generosity, kindness, loyalty, and beyond, and kids can still walk away without any sense of origin, understanding of sin, redemption and salvation, personal relationship with Jesus, or practices of walking in faithfulness to Jesus.

Dominant cultural narratives are like a superstructure that all of life fits within...and so is the gospel. It's actually the only real superstructure among other superstructures. The gospel helps a child understand, God created me. Humans sinned. I've sinned. Jesus is our Savior (and my Savior!). He can restore me to make me more like Him and one day He will make all things fully renewed. Our children need this superstructure (without it they are swimming in a sea of other superstructures). Dr. Albert Mohler of the Southern Baptist Theological Seminary says, "The gospel is the best definition of reality."[12] The gospel is a far more satisfying story. Why? Because it's what's real.

## So That Kids May Believe...

Have you read John chapter 6 lately? If the Bible had a greatest hits album, it very well may be John 6. Check out this list of hit songs: Jesus feeds the five thousand, Jesus walks on water, Jesus as the bread of life, and that controversial B side ballad, eat my flesh and drink my blood. One of my favorite passages in all of Scripture is Peter's response to Jesus' question in John 6:67–69. Here goes:

"You do not want to leave too, do you?" Jesus asked the Twelve.

Then Peter responds,

"Lord, to whom shall we go? You have the words of eternal life. We have come to believe and to know that you are the Holy One of God."

My friend, my brother and sister in Christ, this is what raising kids is all about. This is what coaching and teaching is all about. This is what children's ministry is all about.

As someone who "has a few years" on the kids you are leading, like Peter, you've lived enough to know that our ole friends digital capitalism, hedonism, and the sexual revolution are not delivering on their promises. You understand that the world's systems and narratives have over promised on their allurement and under delivered on their outcomes. And like Peter, you are looking at the kids you minister to, and you are saying, "Kids, what the world is telling you is a lie. It will not satisfy or deliver on its promise. But Jesus will. He has the words of eternal life. Jesus is the one true Holy God. He is life itself and He will lead you to abundant life as you live out the Kingdom of Heaven."

In 1 John 5:13, John says, "I write these things to you who believe in the name of the Son of God, that you may know that you have eternal life." In the very end of the Gospel of John, he writes,

> This is the disciple who is bearing witness about these things, and who has written these things, and we know that his testimony is true.

> Now there are also many other things that Jesus did. Were every one of them to be written, I suppose that the world itself could not contain the books that would be written (John 21:24–25).

Why is Bible engagement important? This is why. Like Peter and John, we want kids to know and believe! We want to point the eyes, ears, minds, hearts, hands, feet, and stomachs—their whole person—to Jesus as the source of life, as abundant life, and as eternal life, and as the King of a better Kingdom. Jesus is our Savior and King and He's the one who brings real renewal (and not the empty promises we hear about through screens and various other ways).

The most foundational factor to influence the formation of lasting faith in children is Bible engagement. As we engage the Bible, we see the Scriptures clearly communicate the Christological story of the gospel. This is what young people need. This is the most foundational way to form the faith of our children.

## Discussion Questions:

1. How frequently do you personally engage the Bible? Consider sharing with one another different ways we engage the Bible, to encourage one another in this area of discipleship practice.

2. Have we evaluated our curriculum through the lens of biblical rigor and appropriateness for children? Furthermore, does our curriculum make the gospel clear on a consistent basis?

3. Do you think the kids in your church understand the "Creation, Fall, redemption, restoration" arch of the Bible? Do the older kids in your children's ministry see this as "reality" and a better option than following the ways of the world?

4. Are there ways where our church (intentionally or unintentionally) uses the Bible Lite Strategy?

5.  Is our ministry a Scripture-rich environment? If not, how can we improve?

## Endnotes

[1] David Kinnaman and Mark Matlock, *Faith for Exiles: 5 Ways for a New Generation to Follow Jesus in a Digital Babylon* (Grand Rapids, Baker Books, 2019), 32.

[2] Kinnaman and Matlock, *Faith for Exiles*, 33.

[3] For more on the Bible Lite Strategy, see here beginning at 19:27: https://www.youtube.com/watch?v=I-nzmVjfbM0.

[4] Christian Smith and Melinda Lundquist Denton, *Soul Searching: The Religious and Spiritual Lives of American Teenagers* (Oxford, Oxford University Press; Reprint edition, 2009).

[5] This definition crafted by Matt Markins and Sam Luce (Child Discipleship Forum, 2022).

[6] Research Project One commissioned by Awana, *5by5 Research Agency* (Nashville, 5by5 Research Agency, 2013), 29.

[7] Research Project One, 28.

[8] Research Project Two, 3.

[9] Research Project Two, 5.

[10] Research Project Two, 4–5.

[11] Research Project Seven, 26.

[12] https://podcasts.apple.com/us/podcast/al-mohler-identity-the-gospel-and-truth-in-todays-culture/id1494535613?i=1000602557986.

# CHAPTER 4

# CULTURE

## Sometimes We Feel Like We're Losing Because of Dominant Cultural Forces

**Shaping the faith of our children takes place in the context of increased, secular cultural formation.**

If this book were a painting, the background of the painting would be secularism and post-Christendom. These are the cultural environments that today's U.S. children are living in (the background). In recent decades in the U.S., the background lighting hasn't always been quite so dark—what changed? This chapter examines that background of secular cultural formation, while the other chapters view the additional seven objects within the painting.

My two sons were born in the early 2000's when the problems of the world that could potentially harm them seemed to be way out there...far away. I lived in a world where I felt I could protect them from the ills and evils of the culture. Then 2007 arrived. Enter iPhone. Then iPad. And apps. And more apps. Steaming services. Video games galore. More screens. Screens while I pump my gas (could I please just have a second to think?!).

What has taken place post-2007 is a rewiring of the systems and infrastructure of the world. Think of our new digital world as an invisible interstate system and each little bit of information, data point, social media post, or video are like invisible cars driving around on the invisible interstate. But instead of being little cars that transport little people, these little invisible cars transport "ideas" and they are transporting them through screens into our minds and hearts. Not just yours and mine, but our children too.

In the 1990s and before, we lived in an illusion that we could somehow build a bubble or mote around little Trevor and Brittany and protect them from the evils of the world. We jammed out to 4Him and Twila Paris CD's, bought our kids "Christian T-Shirts," buckled them up tight in their car seats while they watched Veggie Tales on the portable minivan DVD system.

It was a cultural illusion then, and now we see just how much of an illusion it really was. As much as we as parents and child influencers try to "protect" children from the ideas of secularism, there is no perfect system to adequately shield our children from the never-ending waves of secular ideas. Legalism or moralism will not work. Progressivism certainly isn't the answer. As much as we like filters (and I'm pro filter!) even the best filters don't catch everything. Even at that, if you send your non-smart-phone-child to a social event of any kind (churched or unchurched), he or she will be surrounded by scores of children (some as young as age 7) who have their own smart phone. During these social engagements, all sorts of ideas will be exchanged. Then, suddenly, your bubble-child comes home and asks you about _____ as your face turns five shades of red. How do I respond to this question from my child?! Bubble? What bubble?

As church leaders and parents, here's what we need to grapple with in today's world:

Is my primary motivation to protect children?

*Or*

Is my primary motivation to protect and prepare children?

Protecting our children is not up for negotiation. We. Will. Protect. Children. If we don't protect children, we don't get out of the starting blocks. However, we must go beyond protection; we must prepare them.

Over the last few years Katie and I have helped both of our sons get ready to drive, learn how to drive, survive high school, prepare for college, graduate high school, depart for college, learn how to navigate the online world, thrive in college, learn how to be a good friend, learn how to treat a girl, learn how to be friends with and date a girl, and the list goes on and on. Each one of these was a series of overlapping timelines of never-ending conversation and preparation.

That's just my personal experience, but it's also what we are learning through research. Think of it this way: kids need a running start.

You don't just leap. You get a running start *before* you leap. You don't just ride your bike immediately. You first gain some momentum. You build up to it. In life, you crawl, you waddle, you walk, you jog, you run, you run some more, and now we're getting somewhere. Our sons not only need protecting, but they also need to be prepared. Not just prepared to "survive" in the secular world, but to thrive in their Christian faith in the secular world.

Preparation begins long before the moment they need to "take the leap." You don't just have "the sex talk" one day abruptly with no warning. You start talking about the differences between boys and girls at an early age. The conversation progresses naturally, safely, and age appropriately over a long period of time and before you know it, the conversation takes place naturally at just the right time. You don't just give your kids a smart phone. You start talking about the "whys," social media boundaries, and the impact of mobile technology years before they get a smartphone. You build up to it. You get a running head start. Then you take the leap. If we send kids out into the culture ("take the leap") and we don't prepare them (helping them get a "running head start"), we are setting them up to be pummeled by the never-ending waves of secularism.

Today's kids need to be protected and they also need to be prepared by God's agents of formation, the church, and the home. This preparation begins in childhood in age-appropriate ways. In today's world if we wait until they are in their teen years to begin preparing them to navigate "today's Babylon," we've waited far too long.

One more thing. You may be wondering, why did we spend so much time in the previous chapter about "Bible engagement" discussing the secular culture? One thing I've noticed over the past decade is that many parents and church-es are still communicating with their kids (even when it comes to teaching the Bible) as if it's 1987. We are no longer living in a quasi-majority-Christian-Culture. Much like missionaries going to a distant land who communi-cate the Bible in the native language of the people whom they are engaging, we must embody this missionary-mindset as we raise and disciple kids today. Not just the language, but in context to the cultural assumptions as well. Like the men of Issachar who understood the times and knew what to do, let's prepare our children to bend and flex, but not break under the weight of culture.[1]

This chapter will give us additional insights to inform how we shape the faith of our children in the midst of our new secular background, to thrive in a future culture that many of us may never see. Let's look at the findings.

## Children's Ministry Leaders Lack Confidence in the Influence of the Church

You know how you've thought something dozens of times before, either consciously or subconsciously, but the moment you see it in writing it seems shocking? That's exactly how I feel about this first data point. In our 2022 study with Barna Group, we asked children's ministry leaders,

How Influential do you feel each of the following are on a child's development?[2]

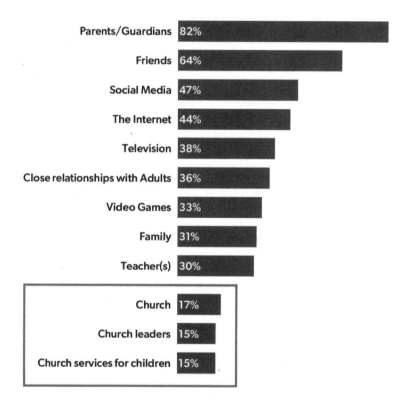

| | |
|---|---|
| Parents/Guardians | 82% |
| Friends | 64% |
| Social Media | 47% |
| The Internet | 44% |
| Television | 38% |
| Close relationships with Adults | 36% |
| Video Games | 33% |
| Family | 31% |
| Teacher(s) | 30% |
| Church | 17% |
| Church leaders | 15% |
| Church services for children | 15% |

Let me go back to my comment about the "shocking" nature of this. In relative terms, 2004 was not all that long ago. That was the year that Sue Miller published her book, *Making Your Children's Ministry the Best Hour of Every Kid's Week*. In just under two decades time, our thinking has shifted from "we can make weekend children's ministry the best hour of a child's week!" to "I'm lacking confidence that the church can influence the development of kids in our ministry."

Why is this? Why has this shift occurred so rapidly?

As local church leaders, we lack confidence that with just one to three hours a week we can have significant influence on the development of children due to all the other factors forming children, such as,

- Screens and mobile technology
- Social anxiety
- Club sports, school sports, and travel sports
- Mental health challenges
- Music, dance, and other extracurriculars
- Ever changing family dynamics
- The sexual revolution
- Video games and social media addiction
- ...and a long list of other items

Going all the way back to Genesis 3, humans have been facing cultural formation. What has changed in recent decades is the intensity. Due to the accessibility to "screens" technology, the secular heat has been turned up. Unlike in past decades, children are no longer sheltered from these items. Rather, now they are in the crosshairs.

This is what we think children's ministry leaders are telling us in the data: When it comes to the overall formation of children, we have a lot to compete with, and we're not sure of our influence.

Here's the thing, I think Sue Miller is right. I think we can make children's ministry the greatest hour of a child's week, but it won't be because of our production value, the skit we worked on so diligently, or the latest children's ministry video. The quality of our Sunday morning production and all the effort we put into that is not the "leading factor" to discipling children in a post-Christian era. The secret is what we discussed in chapters 1, 2, and 3 (combined with some missing links in chapters 5–8). What children need is a community of loving, caring, adult disciple-makers who are highly relational with kids and who find ways to share their faith stories with children—adults who love Jesus, who share the gospel with children, and create a Scripture-rich culture at church and home. We can make children's ministry the greatest hour of a child's week when we place them in highly relational, Scripture-rich environments.

Children's ministry leader, be encouraged. The tools you need to increase your confidence may be right in front of you.

### The Cultural Formation Gap Analysis

In the same 2022 Barna study as above, we asked,

> Do you believe children's ministry should address
> current events, social topics, mental health,
> or potential difficult subjects?[3]

## Parents of 5–14-year-olds:

Yes 75%

No 24%

## Children's Ministry Leaders:

Yes 78%

No 22%

With both parents and those who are responsible for leading local church children's ministries, the overwhelming consensus is that the church cannot ignore the issues forming today's children. We must find ways to appropriately help "prepare" today's kids for not only the world of today, but also the world of tomorrow.

So much has changed culturally since our 2014 study, but when we asked children's ministry leaders about the importance level of developing children who can live for Christ in today's secular culture, the importance level was rated at 4.7.[4] When we asked about the church's performance, the children's ministry community scored our performance as 3.45.[5] That's a gap of –1.25. This was not only one of the larger gaps, but it was also one of the lowest performance ratings (3.45) in the entire survey.

I think this is indicative of the ongoing theme in this chapter: there's a plethora of cultural factors forming today's children and we sense that we lack adequate tools or resources to address the challenge.

What gives me great hope is the Barna Group data above shows that both parents and church leaders agree we have to find ways to address the cultural issues of our day that are forming children. This is a great starting spot! But as we all know (intuitively or by the data), we do have a gap to address (importance vs. performance). A big part of addressing the performance gap on the cultural formation of our children can be found in the final two sections of this chapter and in chapters 5 and 7.

### The More Complex the Issue, the Greater Our Discomfort

I was quite encouraged that in our 2022 Barna Group study 69 percent of children's ministry leaders said they were "very comfortable" at helping children know "how to navigate culture while staying true to their faith."[6] Think about that for a moment, and what a gift that sentence is to the world. Children need help navigating a very complex world, and nearly 7 out of 10 children's ministry leaders are saying "yes" to being up for the challenge! They are very comfortable at the idea of coming alongside of children and helping them to know how to live out their faith in a post-Christian, highly secularized context.

As we drill down into the very same data, however, we do get a clearer picture, and I think what today's children's ministry leader is actually saying is giving us an umbrella statement with two parts underneath:

Umbrella Statement: I'm very comfortable at helping children know how to navigate culture while staying true to their faith

- Within this, there are areas I'm more comfortable with,
- And areas in which I am less comfortable.

Below are the percentages of children's ministry leaders who said "I'm very comfortable leading children at the appropriate age in conversations about…"

## More Comfortable Areas:

| | |
|---|---|
| Use of social media | 60% |
| Technology use | 57% |
| Understanding other cultures | 52% |

## Less Comfortable Areas:

| | |
|---|---|
| Justice issues | 42% |
| Human sexuality | 38% |
| Pornography | 36% |

The story here is, the more complex the issue, the greater our discomfort. I think we have some real exciting opportunities to learn and grow as leaders and parents here, but before I get to my recommendations, let's move into the final section of this chapter on what parents are looking for.

## Parents Are Open to More Help From the Church

I'll be sharing more about parents in chapter 7, but in the context of "cultural formation" we discovered some interesting insights from parents in our 2022 Barna Group study.

A common narrative "about parents" among children's ministry leaders goes something like this, "I try to get parents engaged in discipling their own kids, but all too often, so many parents are disengaged in the process." I understand this narrative...and there is ample data to back this up as being an accurate description for many parents.

At the same time, what I see below is a unique opportunity for us to think differently about "how to capture the attention and imaginations" of parents. Let's check it out.

We were trying to figure out, "Are children's ministries covering the tough topics that matter to parents?"[7] In an effort to understand this, we found that there were three areas where children's ministry leaders seem to be ahead of the game in terms of addressing timely needs. We can think of these as areas where the church is outperforming the expectations of parents. These topics are:

- Bullying
- Loneliness
- Social Media

But there also appears to be some areas where parents believe that children's ministry should address timely cultural items the church seems to be less prepared to address. Below is a comparison of what parents believe should be addressed and what children's ministry leaders report is being addressed on relevant issues.

- Parents of 5–14-year-olds: the percentage who believe children's ministry should address this
- Children's ministry leaders: the percentage who say their ministry has addressed this

## Depression

Parents 55%

Children's Ministry 43%

## Racial Inequality

Parents 48%

Children's Ministry 43%

## Suicide

Parents 47%

Children's Ministry 29%

## Self-harm

Parents 47%

Children's Ministry 28%

## School Shootings

Parents 47%

Children's Ministry 28%

## Sexual Identity

Parents 33%

Children's Ministry 27%

For parents who are already highly engaged in helping their children navigate these complex issues, let me just say: job well done! The world needs more parents like you.

For church leaders, however, I see tremendous opportunity here. As a pastor or leader, you want to see kids reached with the gospel and to be engaged in ongoing discipleship, and you likely get frustrated that more parents are not "stepping up" and leading their own children. Perhaps we can learn from this insight that parents are open to more help from the church.

Consider doing a survey of the parents in your church community. What are their cultural formation concerns? What are the issues they are wrestling with in their home? What challenges are their kids facing? How can you and your church leadership either get equipped or pull in the experts or resources to address the needs the children and families in your church are facing?

I have friends who minister in Africa, and they regularly remind me, "We can't reach a child with the gospel who has a starving stomach. We must first feed them and meet their most basic needs. As we do this, their hearts open up to the love of Jesus." What we can learn from this. What are the "starving stomachs" of our communities? Do parents and kids need help navigating issues relating to sexuality and gender? Do children need help with anxiety or loneliness? What about bullying or social media?

Parents are open to more help from the church. I think church leaders have a tremendous opportunity to discover exactly what the key issues are in your church community and build that bridge to the hearts of parents and children.

### Move From Insight to Action – Three Practical Ideas

Whew. This is a heavy chapter. These are weighty topics. So, what do we do about this? Where do we go from here? I see three opportunities—not only for church leaders, but for parents.

1. **Insight** – We need to gain additional insight as to how the dominant cultures are forming our children, why it's important, and what we can do about it. Insight is incredibly life giving. Insight is like that feeling you get when your best friend says, "You know, when you said _____ to Kelsey, I think you may have made her feel like _____." Suddenly you feel like some greater level of understanding has been achieved. Now you know *why* things are the way they are with you and Kelsey— so now you can do something about it. This is insight. Insight helps us understand the *why* and it takes away the intimidating mystique of something that otherwise might seem daunting. Here's a list of resources that have been incredibly helpful to me and our team in terms of gaining insight in the area of cultural formation. If you haven't come across these yet, I think you will find them insightful as well.

- Listen to *This Cultural Moment Podcast*—Start with Season 1, Episode 1
- Attend the *Child Discipleship Forum*
- Read *Reappearing Church* or *A Non-Anxious Presence* by Mark Sayers
- Read *Faith for Exiles* by David Kinnaman and Mark Matlock
- Read *Our Secular Age* by Collin Hansen (and if you are feeling brave, read *A Secular Age* by Charles Taylor)
- Read *The Rise and Triumph of the Modern Self* by Dr. Carl Trueman

2. **Equipping** – Insight is the starting point, but you need to know what to do about these key insights to bring about change. Here's a few key resources you may find helpful.

- Read *Resilient: Child Discipleship and the Fearless Future of the Church* by Valerie Bell, Mike Handler, and yours truly
- Consider taking your team and key parents from your church to the *Resilient Child Discipleship Training* (Annually, about ten of these are hosted in various cities around the U.S.). This will equip you on "how" to practically make child disciples in the midst of our secular age with proven practices that churches and parents can implement today.
- Read *The Ruthless Elimination of Hurry* by John Mark Comer
- Attend the D6 Conference
- Read *Emotionally Healthy Discipleship* by Pete Scazzero

3. **Practice** – practice is taking our insight and equipping and putting it into action. Here are a few ideas I recommend.

- Start with a discussion with your team on "how do we biblically help children and families who are being formed by the issues of our day?" Do this with your children's ministry team, with a group of parents, or with your small group. Discussion is always a great place to begin. Dialogue and conversation give everyone a chance to express what's in their heart and mind as well as to ask questions and to wrestle with complex issues as a group.
- Pray together with your team and with groups of parents. Just as discussion opens the relational dialogue, channel these questions and anxieties toward the one who can handle them: God. Wrestle with God over these issues. Talk to Him. Plead with Him to give you the wisdom you need that comes from Him. Contend for the children

within and beyond your ministry and home. This is your most important work.

- After attending the *Resilient Child Discipleship Training*, debrief with your team on the key practices you want to implement right away, and discuss how to build these practices into the culture of your church community.

- Roleplay with your leadership team or with a group of parents. Teach one another how to have these complex conversations—how to have them with adults and how to have them with kids (age appropriately and within the right contexts). Roleplay is a great way to put into practice something you may be less comfortable or less familiar with, and a safe way to get experience.

It's becoming more and more clear that the background of our painting has darkened. We are now shaping the faith of our children in the context of increased, secular cultural formation. To you and me, these issues can seem overwhelming and intimidating. Especially when they are no longer "out there" and they are moving closer to the foreground. These are not just issues we discuss in a petri dish—they can be personal, and heavy.

We need insight. We need to get equipped. And we need to get practical so church volunteers, pastors, children's ministry leaders, parents, and grandparents can engage today's children in a way they so desperately need.

Kids need a running start. They need to be prepared. We can't wait until high school. If we wait that long, we've missed the opportunity to give them a running head start, and they will be far more likely to get pummeled by the never-ending waves of secularism. When this happens, many young people fall beneath the waves of culture and never resurface to the faith.

As I breathe in the weight of the moment, I also exhale with the words of Jesus in John 16:33 where He says, "I have said these things to you, that in me you may have peace. In the world you will have tribulation. But take heart; I have overcome the world."

Jesus is going to build His church...and the gates of Hell will not prevail against it.

**Discussion Questions:**

1. Cultural formation is no longer just something that's "out there," it's also in our home communities. When you think about the aspects of

secularism we've discussed in Chapters 3 and 4, how do you see cultural formation impacting children and families in your community? Which aspects do you think you need to name (as you see them shaping children and parents)?

2.  When you think three to five years down the road, which aspects of cultural formation (and how they might form children and families) give you the most concern?

3.  As a church body (church leaders, parents, grandparents, and volunteers), are we adequately preparing kids to thrive in their faith in this not-so-distant future? If not, what might we need to do to begin thinking differently?

4.  For the sake of discussion, if we could temporarily set programs aside (like Sunday School, Large Group, Mid-Week, or VBS as an example), what objectives are the most important to shaping the faith of our children in the midst of our secular age? What if we then took those top three or four objectives and made sure that our programs (Sunday School, Large Group, Mid-Week, or VBS, etc.) were wired to achieve those objectives that are most known to shape lasting faith in children?

5.  What top two or three cultural challenges are parents facing as it relates to discipling children in the secular world? And how can we work church-wide (children's ministry, youth ministry, senior pastor) to address these holistically?

## Endnotes

[1] First Chronicles 12:32, "Of Issachar, men who had understanding of the times, to know what Israel ought to do, 200 chiefs, and all their kinsmen under their command" (ESV).

[2] Research Project Seven, 58.

[3] Research Project Seven, 41.

[4] Research Project Two, 4.

[5] Research Project Two, 6.

[6] Research Project Seven, 39.

[7] Research Project Seven, 42.

# INTERLUDE

You've made it to the interlude. The intermission. The 50-yard line. The half time show. But this halftime show has no fireworks, no stage, no lights, and no "Close your eyes!" kind-of-moments. For you, it's likely a mundane moment, sitting up in bed, relaxing in a chair in your office, lying on the couch, or drinking coffee at a café.

Most of life is this way. Mundane. Like river water flowing over a rock. We are looking down diligently at that rock waiting for something to change. Looking, looking. Truth is, it *is* changing. We just can't see it. Formation happens right before our eyes in the midst of the mundane.

Thus far on our journey together we've been pursuing answers to the question, *"What is it the church does that leads to lasting faith in children?"* I think this is one of the most important questions the church community could be asking and discussing together. As we've stated, it's not a matter of "Are our kids being discipled?" but rather it's a matter of "Whom or what is discipling our kids?"

This is a conversation about *"formation."* The formation of our children is taking place right before our eyes in the midst of the mundane.

*Child discipleship* is the process of joining God in forming children into the image of Jesus Christ as His young disciples. We do our part, and the Holy Spirit does His part. Today's 10-year-old will be leading the church of 2050. We know how fast those mundane days pass by—2050 will be here soon. As responsible leaders we must ask, are we adequately preparing today's kids to lead the church in a future that will likely look quite different from today?

As we ponder this question, we are reminded of why the chief research insights in chapters 1–4 are so incredibly important.

- Our primary shared, desired *outcome* is the lasting faith of our children.
- Loving, caring, adult *relationships* are the most *catalytic* factor in forming the faith of our children.
- Consistent *Bible engagement* is the most *foundational* factor in forming the faith of our children.

- And shaping the faith of our children takes place in the *context* of *increased, secular cultural formation.*

What would it look like for the church community (church leaders and parents) to build our child discipleship pathways around the primary insights most known to lead to lasting faith? Not only would it involve building our ministries around these objectives as the key aims, but it would also involve addressing the gaps we are experiencing in our systems, our infrastructure, and the church cultural norms we currently rely upon.

As we move beyond our interlude—our brief moment of reflection—we will begin to turn our attention to the second half of the book where we will discuss our children's ministry *systems.* Of all topics, why systems? In all our research, not only have we gained insight about "the primary investments that tend to form lasting faith in children," but we've also discovered a considerable amount of insight around "how our systems are often not designed to maximize and impact the area's most known to form lasting faith." So, when it comes to our child discipleship systems, we are facing considerable gaps—and these gaps are preventing us from being most effective at discipling kids in *today's* world (not to mention the future world they will live in that few of us can begin to wrap our minds around).

So, as we move into the second half of our key research findings, the insights we will discuss are time, fun and entertainment, parents, and metrics. As we explore these insights, let's posture our minds and hearts to ask questions like:

- Does the way we spend our time align to our desired objectives of forming lasting faith in children?

- Have we allowed entertainment to play an oversized role in the faith formation of our kids?

- Are we *messaging* to parents that they are responsible for discipling their kids but not actually *showing them how?*

- Do we measure the key factors that are most known to shape lasting faith in children? What if we found a way to begin measuring the areas that actually form a child's faith?

In the introduction, I quoted that humorous but haunting quote attributed to Mark Twain that says, *"It ain't what you don't know that gets you into trouble. It's what you know for sure that just ain't so."* When it comes to our children's ministry systems, the church in the West is at risk of being guilty of this haunting quote. How? Simply by observing our very own actions. As a culture, we have invested significantly into an attractional model of ministry that focuses on "numerical growth" but does significantly less to form deepening faith. We spend massive amounts of time, money, energy, and human capacity on making our weekend experiences and special events more entertaining and fun, but we find ourselves wondering if it's just more entertaining cultural noise. We message to parents that they are responsible for discipling their kids, we give them resources to use, but the resources receive little at-home engagement.

Are these the systems that match what we know to be true about forming the lasting faith of our children? If not, why not build new systems around the things that *are* known to form lasting faith?

As painful as this reality may be, the data is showing us in the West that our systems may be incongruent with our goal of forming lasting faith in children. And this deserves much reflection and dialogue—for what could matter more than the formation of the faith of our children.

# PART 2

# Systems

## The Norms, Processes, Infrastructure, and Culture We Depend on to Form the Faith of Our Children

# CHAPTER 5

# TIME

## The Way Children's Ministry Leaders Spend Our Time Does Not Match Our Desired Objectives

**What if we built our weekly schedule around the ministry investments most known to form lasting faith in children?**

If you were to come to my house, I'm confident you'd notice a couple of details as soon as you stepped in the front door. First, you would see a place designed to feel like home. My wife Katie has done an amazing job turning every house where we've lived into a home. She carefully picks paint colors, we change lighting, I build bookcases, reface fireplaces, or do whatever we can in order to make rooms feel more inviting, and the house feel relaxing and warm. I love it!

The second thing you might notice is how our living room furniture is arranged. We have a sectional and two chairs placed around our fireplace. Why? Because in our home we value conversation and community. I know what you're thinking, and the answer is yes, we also have a TV in there, but it's not the focal point of the room. Our TV happens to be to the side of our fireplace.

The way we arrange the furniture in a room determines how we use that room. We're big readers and in our primary bedroom, we built bookcases and have a small reading nook. Think about the rooms in your home. Think about the furniture you have in those spaces and how it's arranged. Those choices have been made by what you determined to be the most important aspects and activities those rooms facilitate. Maybe your TV is above your fireplace, maybe your kitchen has an island with enough chairs for you and your family to eat at. Whatever choices you made in your own home, you did to fit the priorities of the place.

We can all say the same thing about *time* and how we structure our time to meet certain objectives.

We need to step back and consider doing the same type of intentional design process when we consider how we use our *time* in our ministries. What is taking priority? Have we built our entire structures around one aspect, ignoring other important features of ministry to children that may actually be more impactful and influential?

Perhaps we might have the right principles in place, like having the right furniture choices in a room...but the arrangement is off. Maybe your ministry doesn't need an entire renovation, but small adjustments can compound to make a major difference.

Think about a living room again. If a couch and two chairs were all seated against the same wall, it might be great for watching TV on an opposite wall, but it would be extremely difficult to have a conversation! If you moved and angled the chairs, you would shift your living room from spectating what's on TV to create a community through conversation. As it relates to your ministry to children, you might already have what you need, but you may need to rearrange and make some subtle changes to get better results. Small adjustments to our *time* can lead to major impact through compounding interest! Angle a chair toward a couch and you'll get more conversation. Start giving a bit more time to the relational aspects of your ministry, and you'll begin to see more community and relationship building taking place.

What we will discover in this chapter is we believe as a community that "relational" ministry investments like equipping parents or training volunteers are the most impactful and fruitful ministry investments. Yet, most of our time is spent in "administrative" work, and we spend far fewer hours in actually equipping loving, caring adults to disciple children. It's unanimous—this is grieving us as a community, and we know it's not working.

The answer is not a "complete renovation" strategy. The answer lies in how we make incremental shifts of four percent of our relational ministry equipping time invested to eight percent. Or how do we increase five percent of our relational ministry equipping hours invested to ten percent, or even higher.

First, a little background on how we arrived at this unique moment in time.

## Parents as Primary Spiritual Influence on Their Kids

Prior to the early 2000s, unless you were in a seminary cohort or a rare-hard-to-find-children's-ministry-think-tank, this message of "parents are the primary spiritual influence over their children" wasn't quite the motto of children's ministry as it is today. Don't get me wrong, those of us working in children's ministry in the early 2000s believed this down to our bones. It just wasn't the familiar message quite like it is today. So, in recent history, what was it that popularized this message?

In 2003, George Barna promoted the message through his research published in the book *Transforming Children Into Spiritual Champions: Why Children Should Be Your Church's #1 Priority*. If you happened to be around back then, you remember this was a galvanizing moment. Finally! Someone who gets us! Someone who was able to take what we knew from Scripture (Deuteronomy 6:4–9), plus what we knew intuitively, and added to what we knew experientially—and not to only put it in words, but also to back it up with data. It was a watershed moment for children's ministry, and we are still experiencing the downstream impact of this movement today.[1]

Standing on the shoulders of the 2003 book and research by George Barna came movements, mantras, and methodologies like:

- Church + Home
- Faith @ Home
- The Church-Parent Partnership
- Family Ministry
- Equipping Parents
- Parent Nights
- New Curriculum
- NextGen Ministry
- New Conferences

To be clear, these are each very good and valiant ministry efforts! Central to each of these are two components: 1) Resourcing parents and 2) Equipping parents (we will unpack the nuances that make these two components uniquely distinct throughout this chapter and in chapter 7).

So when it comes to resourcing, if we could use our own trade as a metaphor for ourselves, we'd say this: The take-home paper found its way to the floor of the minivan. A common narrative from many children's ministry leaders is the church is resourcing the parents, but the parents are not using the resources. Why is this?

As we will see in data in the sections ahead, we have been quick to resource parents, but slow to equip and train them.

Early on in marriage, Katie and I were both in ministry and we didn't even have two nickels to rub together. So, I did what any honorable husband would do, I started delivering pizzas as a part-time job. When I was hired on as a pizza delivery boy, I had to go through a cheesy training (pun intended). The goofy videos. The role playing. It was awkward. Yet, I knew just what to do. I wasn't lacking in clarity. I obtained the information. I saw it demonstrated. I was able to participate in the process of some of the key tasks I was going to be asked to perform. When you get your mind, hands, feet, mouth, and emotions involved, it tends to stick with you.

I think back on this often as I hear a children's ministry leaders grieve the lack of engagement from parents. I find myself wondering, but are they equipped? Do they understand the vision? Has someone modeled this for them over coffee or in a participatory environment? Have we trained them? Have they been able to roleplay in a safe place where they can mess up, laugh, feel embarrassed, yet also learn, "Hey! I can do this!"?

The research shows we know this. We know the most fruitful way to build a children's ministry is to make relational investments into loving, caring adults like parents and volunteers. According to the self-reported data, however, we're just not doing it frequently.

Let's take a look at some of the most insightful findings in all the research we've commissioned.

## Administrative Tasks Dominate Our Weekly Schedule

This past year, my wife came across a YouTube channel called, *The Behavior Panel.* Have you seen these guys? The channel consists of four behavioral experts whose occupational craft and discipline has to do with studying human behavior like facial expressions, nonverbal gestures, body movement, use of language, tone, mood, etc. Collectively, these guys have consulted with U.S. military, FBI, CIA, celebrities, criminals, and global leaders. On their YouTube channel they analyze clips of high-profile court cases or blockbuster interviews in the media. Clip by clip, they will make the rounds each evaluating a person's body language with the motivation of answering the questions, "Is this person being honest? Or are they being deceptive?" Their job is not to determine if someone is guilty or not guilty—they are simply trying to detect truthfulness or deception based on what we know to be true about human body language. Hint: managers and parents, this channel is a gold mine!

One thing these guys have taught us is the importance of establishing a "behavioral baseline" in terms of each person's human behavior. Your baseline behavior is you when you are relaxed. Your baseline defines your behavioral reality—your normal posture, normal facial expressions, normal voice tone, etc. Just you, being you. Then, these behavioral experts compare each subsequent clip back to the baseline. It's fascinating stuff.

One important aspect in our 2022 research project on "how children's ministry leaders spend their time" has to do with understanding our behavioral baseline. In order to establish this baseline, we asked children's ministry leaders this open-ended question:

As a children's ministry leader in your church, how do you spend your time each week? Please list the top items that fill up the majority of your calendar each week:[2]

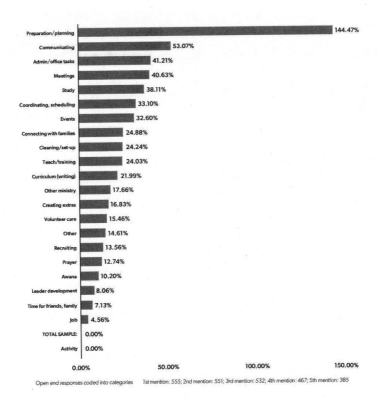

Total sample broken down by order of mention

Preparation/planning – 144.47%

This was such an insightful way to help us understand our baseline—the default way we are naturally spending our time each week. Not, how would you like to spend your time? Or what is the best way you could spend your time? Simply, give me the baseline. Define reality on how your time is spent.

Notice in this open-ended question, we gave the respondents up to five opportunities to respond. The 5by5 Research Agency then went through each of the mentions and coded them based on the meaning of the response. Right away what we observed is that there was a clear top response of Preparation or Planning, scoring a whopping 144.47 percent. How can that be? That's because each person (remember, multiple mentions) mentioned "preparation or planning" about 1.44 times on average. But wait, there's more.

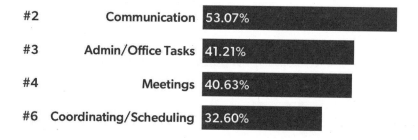

In an effort of helping us understand our baseline in terms of "time spent," we spend the vast majority of our time doing administrative work that involves preparing, planning, coordinating, scheduling, office tasks, communication, and meetings. In Luke 14:28, Jesus Himself gives a nod to administrative and planning work when He says, "Suppose one of you wants to build a tower. Won't you first sit down and estimate the cost to see if you have enough money to complete it?" (NIV). In Acts 6, we observe a division of labor between those who will serve widows through food distribution (administrative tasks) compared to those who are dedicated to prayer and the teaching of the Word.

Without planning, our gatherings would be a train wreck. Without communication, there is no clarity. Your administrative work involves important tasks.

The question in front of us is one of wisdom and stewardship. I'm not questioning whether our time should be used for administrative purposes (nor do I hear anyone else questioning that). It was obvious in Acts 6 that the widows needed served in the distribution of the food, and it's obvious today that our planning and preparation are essential to facilitate our ministries and organizations.

What I am questioning, and what we all need to question is the dominance these items have as they take over nearly every hour of our calendar. Let me illustrate through an embarrassing story.

A few years back, Katie came to me and said, "We haven't been on a date in six months. Why is that?" Being who I am, I quickly resorted to rationalization of this event and that event, this trip and that trip, our two sons' busy schedules, blah, blah, blah. At the end of my explanation, Katie kindly repeated her question. There was no getting out of this, I was guilty. Katie's point was, yeah, yeah, life is always going to be busy. We make time for what is most important.

Remember the "rocks in the jar" illustration? Budgeting the time on our calendar is a lot like that. We place the big rocks in the jar first, then the medium rocks, the small rocks, and lastly the sand fills in all the cracks. I had left the big rock of nurturing and cultivating my relationship with Katie out of the jar. Yikes!

When it comes to children's ministry, I'm questioning, what *should* be our big rocks in terms of time invested weekly? And according to the data, you are asking the same question.

## Biggest Ministry Impact Areas Get the Least of Our Time

Picking up where we left off in the previous section, in that same 2022 study, we asked,

> Of the activities listed below, which ones would you say
> take up the majority of your time and capacity
> throughout a typical week?[3]

**Select up to five.**

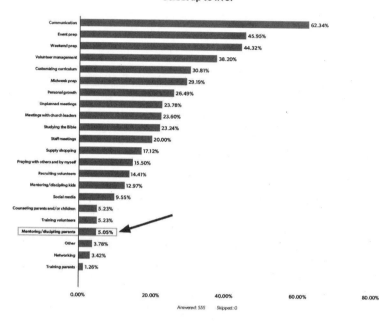

Communication 62.34%
Event prep 45.95%
Weekend prep 44.32%
Volunteer management 38.20%
Customizing curriculum 30.81%
Midweek prep 29.19%
Personal growth 26.49%
Unplanned meetings 23.78%
Meetings with church leaders 23.60%
Studying the Bible 23.24%
Staff meetings 20.00%
Supply shopping 17.12%
Praying with others and by myself 15.50%
Recruiting volunteers 14.41%
Mentoring/discipling kids 12.97%
Social media 9.55%
Counseling parents and/or children 5.23%
Training volunteers 5.23%
Mentoring/discipling parents 5.05%
Other 3.78%
Networking 3.42%
Training parents 1.26%

0.00%    20.00%    40.00%    60.00%    80.00%

Answered: 555    Skipped: 0

Notice this was not an open-ended question, rather in this question we gave the respondents options to choose from. Once again, the vast majority of the top responses were items like communication, event preparation, weekend preparation, curriculum customization, midweek prep, church leader meetings, and even unplanned meetings.

Regardless of whether it's an open-ended question, or a question with pre-selected options, the story is consistent: Administrative work dominates our weekly schedule. But let's not stop there. Let's push in to understand the areas of our time investment we believe have the biggest ministry impact.

In this same 2022 study, we asked,

> Regardless of how you spend the majority of your time,
> what are you doing that you believe will have
> the most impact on child discipleship?[4]

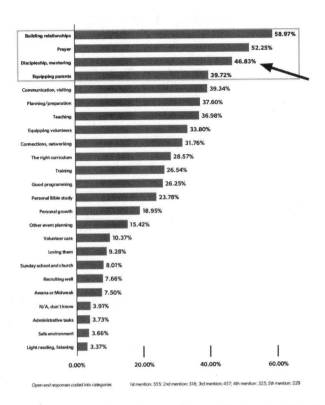

| | |
|---|---|
| Building relationships | 58.97% |
| Prayer | 52.25% |
| Discipleship, mentoring | 46.83% |
| Equipping parents | 39.72% |
| Communication, visiting | 39.34% |
| Planning/preparation | 37.60% |
| Teaching | 36.98% |
| Equipping volunteers | 33.80% |
| Connections, networking | 31.76% |
| The right curriculum | 28.57% |
| Training | 26.54% |
| Good programming | 26.25% |
| Personal Bible study | 23.78% |
| Personal growth | 18.95% |
| Other event planning | 15.42% |
| Volunteer care | 10.37% |
| Loving them | 9.28% |
| Sunday school and church | 8.01% |
| Recruiting well | 7.66% |
| Awana or Midweek | 7.50% |
| N/A, don't know | 3.91% |
| Administrative tasks | 3.73% |
| Safe environment | 3.66% |
| Light reading, listening | 3.37% |

0.00%    20.00%    40.00%    60.00%

Open end responses coded into categories    1st mention: 555; 2nd mention: 516; 3rd mention: 457; 4th mention: 325; 5th mention: 229

Just for a moment, think back on what we discussed in chapter 1: Lasting faith is the desired outcome. Reaching kids with the gospel and leading them into a discipleship relationship with Jesus is our heartbeat. As children's ministry leaders and highly engaged parents, it's what we are aiming for!

Notice the sharp contrast between the open-ended responses in the previous section where we were simply establishing a behavioral baseline, compared to these responses here. The top four responses that children's ministry leaders believe have the "the most impact on child discipleship" are:

- Building Relationships – 58.97%
- Prayer – 52.25%
- Discipleship/Mentoring – 46.83%
- Equipping Parents – 39.72%

These are followed closely by communication/visiting (39.34%), teaching (36.98%), equipping volunteers (33.80%), and connections/networking (31.76%). What do you notice about the top 10 open-ended responses?

Eight of the top ten open-ended responses to what has the greatest impact on child discipleship are overtly relational in nature.

Houston, we have a gap. Let's talk more about that gap—especially as it relates to parents.

In this same study, near the end of the survey, we asked this open-ended question, "What do you wish you could do (that you are not currently doing) in any of these areas in this survey to be more effective in discipling children?"[5] The top two responses were:

- Mentor or Equip Parents – 25.68%
- Equip Volunteers – 20.72%

Coming in at a distant third place was "more resources" (10.45%) and in fourth place was "more time" (8.83%).

More time.

On a Monday morning when we glance ahead at our schedule, we see a week packed with planning, preparation, events, coordination, and administrative tasks. We value this work. It's important. At the same time, our eyes glance over to that one lone coffee appointment with a parent and we long for more relational opportunities to engage with loving, caring, adult child disciple-makers.

As children's ministry leaders, we know that the most fruitful way to disciple children is to relationally equip and mentor volunteers and parents. According to how our time is spent, however, our church culture and system is simply not wired that way.

Let's take a look at exactly how much relational time we are getting with parents—with the intention of training, mentoring, and equipping them to disciple their own children.

## The Gap Between Our Message and Methods

Let's face it, this whole chapter is a gap analysis. It's a gap analysis between:

| What we say is important to us: | How we spend our time: |
|---|---|
| Parents are the primary spiritual influence over their children. | Mostly administrative and few hours spent equipping parents |

It's been 20 years since George Barna's book and research was published that helped popularize the narrative *parents are the primary spiritual influence over their children.* It's a fair question to ask, how have we equipped them to steward their influence with their children? How have we trained them to maximize that impact? In this same 2022 study, we asked:

How frequently are you focusing specifically
on equipping parents to help them disciple
their children in any way?[6]

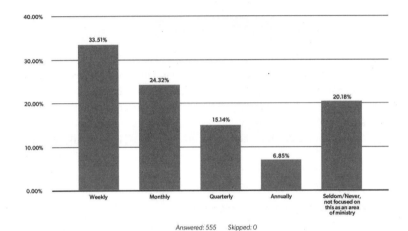

Answered: 555    Skipped: 0

The first thing our team noticed was that one in five of those in children's ministry seldom or never spend time equipping parents to disciple their children. When we asked this segment why they do not spend their time equipping parents, the top three open-ended responses were, Not an area of focus (27.43%), Uninterested parents (21.24%), and Time restraint (16.81%).[7] What we see here from this group is that for one in five churches, equipping parents is not a part of their plan, they are spending their time on other areas, and even if they were to spend their time on this, they believe parents are just not going to step up.

Let's now drill into the segment of children's ministry leaders that are the *most frequently* engaged in equipping parents—those who report spending time equipping parents *weekly.* We asked them, "On average, how many hours per week are you engaged in equipping parents?"[8]

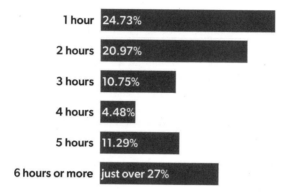

This group only represents one in three children's ministry leaders and when it comes to equipping parents, they are the high performers among us. They are the most engaged at equipping parents on a weekly basis, and the majority of this segment (just over 55% of this group) are spending 1–3 hours per week equipping parents to disciple their children. From here, it drops off swiftly.

- *Monthly,* most do so 1–5 hours a month.[9]

- *Quarterly,* most do so 1–6 hours a quarter.[10]

- *Annually,* most do so 1–4 hours a year.[11]

It's time for us to sit back and take a deep breath. Inhale. Exhale. Again...

Ok, let's think together about the logical flow of what we've just consumed together in this chapter. First, we believe that forming lasting faith is the desired outcome of children's ministry. Second, the children's ministry community has adopted the mantra of "parents are the primary spiritual influence over their children." Third, we believe the most impactful use of our time (to disciple children) is to invest relationally in equipping parents and volunteers who are on the front lines of discipling children. Finally, fourth, we spend the vast majority of our time in administrative tasks and very little relational time in equipping parents.

Like a trellis to a vine, so much of our administrative work provides real value to our ministry. Yet, we grieve the fact that only a small fraction of our time is spent in what we believe is the most fruitful work at discipling children—which is relational investments in equipping loving, caring adults who can disciple children.

The question in front of us is one of wisdom and stewardship. If we want to maximize forming the faith of our children, what would be the wise thing for the church community to do? How can we steward our time most wisely to form the faith of our children?

**Relational Compound Interest: Moving From 5% to 10%**

I'm not an expert on compound interest. However, I know enough that when it comes to retirement investing, slight percentage increases combined with a longer duration of time invested can yield exponential growth and impact. Let's say I'm investing five percent of my income into a 401k. Even increasing that investment to seven percent or ten percent over the course of 25 years, 30 years, and especially 40 years will yield significantly higher returns over time.

The answer to attaining more relational equipping time with parents and volunteers is a "non-negotiable slight percentage tweak" to our calendar (time investment). For those who are investing in their retirement, they set aside the seven percent, the ten percent, or the 15 percent investment *first* (it can even come out of your paycheck pre-tax). This is a non-negotiable, first priority kind of decision.

In a similar way, sort of like the illustration where we put the big rocks in the jar first, we solve our shared problem that we've discussed in this chapter by making the "non-negatable decision" that we will invest (x increased) hours a week in the relational equipping of parents and volunteers per (week, month, quarter, year). Then we build the rest of our schedule around this. What could this look like?

Taking the data segments from this chapter, it could look a bit like this below for those who invest in relational equipping of parents weekly, monthly, quarterly, or annually:

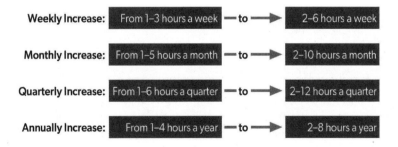

Much like how our retirement percentage comes out of our paycheck first (pre-tax), blocking this time on our calendars needs to be non-negotiable. We put this on our calendar first, then everything else must work around this. Why? We have a wisdom and stewardship issue. Wisdom is telling us that this investment of our time is the most fruitful way to steward our gospel and discipleship impact to shape the future of the church.

Having been in the realm of children's ministry and child discipleship for over 20 years, I've concluded that if we don't make increased relational equipping of parents and volunteers a non-negotiable in how we spend our time, we will continue to share the "parents are the primary" message but in terms of action, few will be trained and equipped.

Parents need inspiration and vision.

Parents need equipping, training, mentorship, community, and experience.

Parents need to be discipled.

If we cling to our existing culture and system, it's unlikely we will see much change.

**Discussion Questions:**

1. What distinct role does the church (pastors, kids ministry leaders, volunteers, etc.) have in discipling children in the church community? What distinct role do parents (and caregivers) have in discipling the children within their care? Are these roles and responsibilities clear within your church community?

2. Does your church community have the awareness that most people come to Christ between the ages of 4–14? Does your church community have the awareness that worldview is largely shaped in most people by the age of 13?

3. What's your baseline? How do you spend your time each week? What takes up the majority of your time?

4. Just like you would prioritize your tithe (giving) first or your retirement investing first, what would it look like to schedule out relational equipping on your calendar? Weekly? Monthly? Quarterly? Annually? How might this help you and your church to cast vision with parents and to equip them to disciple their kids?

5.  When you do (or will) meet with parents, what are the best formats or methodologies for relational equipping? Casual one-on-one visits over coffee? Small group informal discussions? Formal trainings? Big events? Or some combination?

## Endnotes

[1] Also check out George Barna's follow-up to this book called *Revolutionary Parenting: What the Research Shows Really Works* published in 2007.

[2] Research Project Eight commissioned by Awana, *5by5 Research Agency* (Nashville, 5by5 Research Agency, 2022), 103.

[3] Research Project Eight, 104.

[4] Research Project Eight, 105.

[5] Research Project Eight, 129.

[6] Research Project Eight, 106.

[7] Research Project Eight, 111.

[8] Research Project Eight, 107.1.

[9] Research Project Eight, 108.1.

[10] Research Project Eight, 109.1.

[11] Research Project Eight, 110.1.

# CHAPTER 6

# FUN

## When It Comes to Having Fun, We Are Outperforming Our Own Expectations

**Kids are fun, and kid's ministry is fun: But have we unknowingly given entertainment and relevance too much priority in our kid's ministry?**

When I think about "summertime" in my childhood in the 1980s, I think of one word: fun. Ok, more than fun: it was pure delight! We'd play whiffle ball in the back yard, run in packs from house-to-house, pick-up basketball games, raiding the neighbor's pantry, sleepovers, watching way too much TV, and late nights at the Little League baseball diamond where we heard "please return all foul balls to the concession stand for a free snow cone" and raced to be the first to get that ball. For me, summertime was the apex of childhood fun.

When I think of my two sons' childhoods in the 2000s, I see these same themes: fun, bliss, delight. Their curiosity, their playfulness, their wonder, their laughter, their hunger to learn and explore. This is the universal truth about children: wherever you go in the world, you will see kids finding endless, creative ways to have fun.

So it's no surprise that *fun* plays a key role in the faith formation of our children: At church, at home, and in all of life. When we study this history of children and youth ministry, we see that fun has played a key role in Sunday School, children's church, Christian youth programs, Christian school clubs, church camps, children's ministry curriculum...all the way through the numerous innovations to where we are today.

Fun is here, and it's here to stay, because it's a part of who children are and how they learn, grow, and develop. What we will explore in this chapter is, what role should fun play in our ministry, and what are we using to fuel it? It's going to play a role, but what do we want that role to be?

True confession, without this research it would have been easy for me to miss this, if it were not for an unavoidable *outlier* in our research. An outlier is a data point that differs or stands out from the rest. In all our research, "fun" has been an interesting criterion because according to the research it's the one area we care about the least but perform the best. Sort of like scanning down a report card and every box is checked "has not met expectations" and then suddenly there is only one box (the outlier) that's checked "exceeds expectations." When you look to see the category it's *fun!*

Think about a children's ministry conference you may have attended in the past (the kind that has the big expo center with all the booths in the exhibit hall). When you think about the vendors and organizations who are in attendance, what is woven into many of the products, programs, and widgets being represented on the expo floor? Within children's ministry, there's a strong current of "entertainment" or "relevance" in these offerings so kids in our ministries have fun. A high percentage of what's on the exhibit hall floor is designed to "pump more fun" into our local church children's ministry.

Once again, kids are fun. Fun is here, and it's here to stay. No one is arguing otherwise (Okay, maybe the Amish? I'm not sure). What must be evaluated is the role fun plays within our ministry, and what we are using to fuel it. To give us a visual image,

If fun was a fire,
what logs do we use to fuel the fun fire?

In this chapter we will think critically as we evaluate, have we unknowingly given entertainment and relevance too much priority in forming the faith of our children? Let's get started.

## Goofy or Real

Have you ever had one of those caricatures drawn of you, a close friend, or a family member? One of those cartoon sketches that takes your striking features and exaggerates them a bit. The thing about caricatures is they are exaggerated, but they *are* based off a source. When I see myself in a caricature with my pointy nose enlarged, my high cheek bones lifted, and my brow accentuated, I begin to think, "Hey wait a minute!" only to be reminded, oh, I do have a pointy nose, high cheek bones, and a brow like a bookshelf. I find a caricature of myself to be goofy—not something that I take all that seriously.

The reality is caricatures are goofy. In the world of politics, they are used to make a subtle point. A soft jab. Not to be taken too seriously. We see this entertaining "goofy" effect in other parts of life as well. Consider these two images below:

As we think about children's ministry—not only the last 50 years but also in our current moment—it's possible we may be giving children an entertaining caricature at a cultural moment when the world is giving them "what's real."

Caricatures are goofy, and real is, well, real. You and I know the caricature of Noah's ark is based off something real (sort of like my bookshelf-brow) according to the Scriptures. But in a child's mind, if the church is giving them "some goofy caricature" and the school system is giving them the "Science is what's real and true" message backed up with all sorts of "irrefutable data," how could we expect that child to take the church seriously as that child grows and matures and has deeper questions? Will he/she consider the church to be a place where you turn to in order to ask life's big questions?

Let's move away from the caricature of Noah's ark but apply the idea in other areas of children's ministry.

Like me, you've evaluated enough children's ministry videos, songs, dramas, curriculum, books, and various forms of other entertainment and teaching support to know there's a plethora of goofy or silly resources out there to aid in forming the faith of our children. I'd like to repeat what I mentioned earlier,

> If fun was a fire,
> what logs do we use to fuel the fun fire?

Kids are fun, and play is part of their nature. I would even argue that goofy and silly are some of the logs in the fun fire. But to what degree? When I step back and look at children's ministry at large, I'm questioning, of all the logs in the fun fire, have we put too many goofy and entertaining logs in the fun fire in an attempt to be relevant, only to end up being irrelevant in the end?

Like that child whose eyes are glancing back and forth between the Noah's ark caricature and the picture of the cosmos taken by a satellite camera, that child is wondering, what's real? What is life really all about, and who can help me figure that out?

As a pastors, kids pastors, and influential parents, it's our job to think through what logs we want to use to fuel the fun fire, and how many of each to strike the right balance at effective child discipleship. Like a caricature, entertainment is a thing not to be taken too seriously. If our ministry to children gets too many entertainment logs in the fun fire, we simply end up becoming the caricature—a thing not to be taken too seriously.

## Outlier, Outlier, Pants on Fire

In our 2014 study we asked this open-ended question, "Thinking about what children's ministry in a church should accomplish, what would you say is the most important purpose or objective of children's ministry in a church?[1]

To no surprise to anyone, the top three responses were *evangelize* (50.72%), *disciple* (38.25%), and *teach* (33.30%). The story here in the data is the ongoing story of "go and make disciples." To make disciples of children we introduce them to Jesus, we lead them to Jesus, and we disciple them by teaching them to follow Jesus.

However, near the very bottom of the list of responses from children's ministry leaders was "fun" at 2.1 percent. Fun made the list, but it's not on the top of the vast majority of children's ministry leaders minds when they think about the purpose of their children's ministry.

In that same project we asked,

> Thinking about the purpose or objective of your church's children's ministry programming, for each of the following statements describing a purpose or objective, first of all tell how important you believe the purpose/objective is. Please answer using a 5-point scale where 1 is "not important at all" and 5 is "very important."[2]

> Helping children enjoy their church experience—have fun

> Importance – 4.29

Then we asked,

> Next, tell how you believe your church's children's ministry overall
> is fulfilling each purpose/objective. Please answer using a 5-point
> scale where 1 is "not fulfilling at all" and 5 is "fulfilling completely."[3]
>
> Helping children enjoy their church experience—have fun
>
> Performance – 3.95

Here's where the outlier comes in. In this particular project, nowhere was
there a greater contrast in the research between a) What's important to children's ministry leaders and b) What we are doing. Consider this:

Fun ranked as the least
important objective out
of 10 areas evaluated ↓

Fun scored as our
↑ highest ranking in
terms of what we do
(our performance)

One way to think of this is how I viewed P.E. class in high school (Sorry Mr.
Drake): I viewed P.E. as the least important class, but it was also the one in
which I got the best grade.

When we just look at the data, and ask, what are we most effective at? According to children's ministry leaders, we are most effective at helping children
enjoy their church experience by having *fun*. Our gap here was only a –0.34
which means we're almost giving ourselves a perfect score.

This same project contained qualitative interviews and one of the overarching ideas in the focus groups was this: we are afraid we may have sacrificed
substance for fun and entertainment. Here's a few of the actual comments
shared in the focus groups:

- "Giving place to the Holy Spirit to do His work...not getting so caught
  up in the 'program' and the fun that we give no place for God to work."
- "Children want to have fun...but you have to teach the gospel. A big
  challenge I face is combining the two. Teaching the gospel in a way
  kids can connect and still have fun. That they would enjoy learning
  about Jesus."
- "I think more often than not children's ministry is more babysitting
  and fun than teaching children discipleship. How can we change this?"

You can sense the tension in these comments. Of course, children's ministry
is going to be fun—kids are fun! Yet, the gravitas that we've given fun and

entertainment in children's ministry is an outlier. When it comes to fun, our pants are on fire, and we are uncomfortable. We don't see fun and entertainment as being the highest objectives, but it is what we do best.

## Consider the Culture

Our current map (or model) of children's ministry was being blueprinted back in the 1970s–1990s (which then got published and popularized in the 2000s). During that time in the U.S., we were living in a quasi-Christian culture. This means that Christianity had a seat at the mainstream cultural table. The Bible was a generally respected book, the church held a place of prominence within the community, pastors were generally respected, Jesus was a positive historical figure, and Billy Graham was the ideal human being. Now, there were places like Portland, Boston, and San Francisco where the U.S. was already well down the path toward a post-Christian culture, but for much of the U.S. the shift sped up only within the past decade. Let's think about this for a moment,

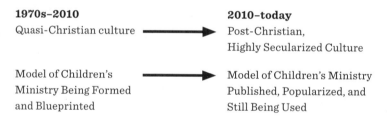

**1970s–2010**
Quasi-Christian culture

**2010–today**
Post-Christian,
Highly Secularized Culture

Model of Children's
Ministry Being Formed
and Blueprinted

Model of Children's Ministry
Published, Popularized, and
Still Being Used

The model of children's ministry that has been popularized and that most churches are using today, was blueprinted with high values on entertainment and fun. It was designed to form and reach children in a culture that no longer exists. We are no longer living in a quasi-majority Christian culture where the mainstream values and narratives support Christian thinking. We are now living in a highly secularized culture where we are grappling with childhood issues like:

- Loneliness and isolation
- Screen addiction
- Increased childhood anxiety
- Biblical illiteracy
- Gender dysphoria
- Two years of disrupted education due to Covid-19
- Social media and video game addiction

- Single parent homes
- School shootings
- ...just to name a few

Anxiety is the "check engine light" for our society. The child and youth anxiety epidemic is like the little blinking light on the dashboard saying, there's a problem, and it's a symptom of a larger problem. Secularism is failing our children, and the church has an unprecedented opportunity to meet this moment with something far more satisfying with what the world is offering them.

While our kids are trying to stay above the water line of the pounding waves of the secular cultural, the church must face this outlier: the thing we value the least is the thing we do the best. We are good at fun and entertainment. So good, that we are outperforming our own expectations. Not only that, the publishers and media companies are hyper-creative, and they have a gift of giving us an unending supply of entertainment logs to stoke the fun fire.

Kids are fun. Fun is here, and it's an essential part of how they learn. We must evaluate, however, how do we stoke the fun fire? As pastors, kids' pastors, and influential parents, we must think critically about what logs we want to use to fuel the fun fire, and what role those play in forming the faith of our children. Do we need more entertaining, relevant, and cool-Christianity? Or in this cultural moment, do our kids need something different? In a world of mass cultural confusion, is there a different type of fun engagement that our children are looking for?

I keep thinking back on that child who is glancing back and forth between the caricature of Noah's ark and the picture of the cosmos taken by a satellite camera. What does this child need from the church? How can we engage today's child not only in a way that is fun, but in a way that answers his deep questions and longings? We don't want to be like a caricature—doubling down on entertainment and relevance and out of sync with our cultural moment only to find we've become a thing not to be taken too seriously.

**Discussion Questions:**

1. Is "fun" a stated value in your children's ministry? Or is it an assumed value in your ministry? To what degree do you and your team value fun?

2. Specifically what role or objective does fun play in your children's ministry? How does fun help you form the faith of the children in your home or ministry?

3. Using the "fun fire" analogy, what logs do you use to fuel fun? (E.g., games, media, videos, etc.) How do you believe these methods are contributing to the faith formation of the children in your care?

4. How would your team answer this question, "Of all the logs in the fun fire, have we put too many goofy and entertaining logs in the fun fire?"

5. In a world of excess entertainment for children, what do you think your children need most in terms of engagement from adults in your church community?

**Endnotes** ———————————————————

1 Research Project Two, 23.

2 Research Project Two, 3.

3 Research Project Two, 5.

# CHAPTER 7

# PARENTS

## Parents Are the Primary Influence Over Their Children but Are Less Engaged in Discipling Them

**What if churches formed a true partnership with parents that equips them to disciple their kids based on their capacities and capabilities?**

Reality TV became mainstream in the early 2000s and has remained one of the most popular forms of television and streaming content. We are curious about watching the lives of other people. We seem to like to watch normal people doing normal things as well as extraordinary things. We also like watching famous people doing normal things and famous people doing extraordinary things—and everything in between!

Our affinity for "reality" TV is telling us something about our inescapable quest for...reality. (Spoiler alert, much of reality TV is scripted.) Yet, the concept behind reality TV is this idea that what we are seeing is real, or at least close to real. Whether it's Alaska, Great Britain, Waco, Texas, or the Jersey Shore, our culture tends to crave it.

Using the concept behind reality TV for a moment, let's use our imaginations once again. What if we could follow the lives of 15 randomly selected "church-going" young people from a church in the U.S.? Using this imaginary scenario, what would we learn about their school life, their home life, and their extra curriculars? Digging a little deeper, I'd want to know, do they feel seen, known, and loved? Do they have a sense of belonging? Is there someone who is regularly getting time with them? Is there someone watching over them with a sense of protection and care? Are they receiving eye contact, conversation, and making good relational connection? And specifically, as a follower of Jesus, I'd want to know, are they engaging the Bible? Are they being discipled? Is someone showing them how to love and follow Jesus?

I suspect what we'd discover is our 15 church-going children and students have parents that fall into one of four categories:

- **Higher-Capacity Parents** – These parents are highly engaged in discipling their own children. They are disciples of Jesus themselves, and they are intentional about discipling their own children.

- **The Occasional Parents** – These parents engage in discipling their children from time to time. They are well meaning, inconsistent, and not intentional when it comes to discipling their children. They love Jesus and at the same time just kind of go with the cultural flow.

- **Less-Engaged Parents** – These parents usually don't move from A to Z. They need someone to help them understand, 1) How far they can go (what is their capacity to grow?) and 2) Help them grow and progress (e.g., A to G) in taking steps of spiritual responsibility.

- **The Not-Gonna-Happen Parents** – The reality is, there are some parents who simply will not engage in discipling their own children. Even though they attend church, perhaps they themselves are not a disciple of Jesus? Or they may simply lack spiritual maturity, are overwhelmed, are distracted, or they could be carrying so much pain and woundedness that they are not able to be a spiritual parent. For a variety of reasons, this group does not engage, no matter how hard the church tries to equip or inspire them.

Based on what we already know about parental engagement from the Fuller Youth Institute, Barna Group, Christian Smith, and others, a high percentage of parents will have minimal engagement and many simply will not engage at all. Therefore, our imaginary scenario of 15 kids may look a bit like this:

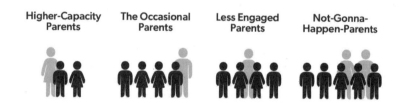

| Higher-Capacity Parents | The Occasional Parents | Less Engaged Parents | Not-Gonna-Happen-Parents |

The fewest number of children live in homes with higher-capacity parents (as it relates to discipling their children), followed closely by parents who occasionally engage in discipling their children. A larger group of children live in homes with less-engaged parents (as it relates to discipling their children), and the largest group of children live in homes where child discipleship is

simply not going to take place at home. These parents are just busy, distracted, have elevated other priorities, perhaps they are hurting, or for whatever
reason they simply are not going to engage in discipling their own children.

This scenario, although imaginary, illustrates these five strategic thoughts
that child disciple-makers must grasp:

1.  The starting point in a *children's ministry mindset* is often the weekly
    church programming and events. This approach begins with church
    programming in mind (Large Group/Small Group, Sunday School,
    Children's Church, etc.) and aims to make the programming effective
    for as many children as possible during a weekend church service.

2.  The starting point in a *child discipleship mindset* is the child and the
    child's weekly environment. This approach begins with the child in
    mind and puts a discipleship plan in place (at church and at home)
    based on the child's needs and environment.

3.  To most fruitfully and faithfully disciple children, the church must
    have a true *partnership* with parents. This involves coming alongside
    of parents based on where each parent is on their journey by equip-
    ping them on how to engage in discipling their children based on their
    capacities and capabilities.

4.  When a child lives in a "not-gonna-happen" parental environment, the
    church takes on the role and posture of maximizing every discipleship
    moment possible with that child to help them grow as a young disciple
    of Jesus Christ.

5.  A *child discipleship mindset* will cause us to ask, "How can we design
    our children's ministry to equip parents to disciple each child based
    on their unique situation? And how can we maximize every moment
    possible to disciple children at church while we have the opportunity
    to shape their faith?"

As Westerners, we tend to think size and scale as our *starting point*. It's
the initial starting assumption that influences much of our conscience and
subconscious thinking. Therefore, when we think about leading a "children's
ministry" our starting assumption relates to scale, growth, and expansion.
Thinking in terms of mass or scale is necessary (The feeding of the 5,000, the
explosion of the church in Acts, Moses and Jethro, etc.). At the same time,
we must *also* think in terms of diverse uniqueness: meaning, not all of the
children or parents within the "mass" are the same (e.g., the four groups of
parents mentioned above). Therefore, our approach to equipping a particular

parent or connecting with a specific child must be designed to meet them where they are on their own development pathway to help them take steps forward on their discipleship journey.

To form the faith of our children, the church must form a true partnership with parents based on their capacities and capabilities that equips them to disciple their kids.

### Why Do Young People Leave the Church?

Starting with the end in mind, in our 2022 project with Barna Group, we asked both children's ministry leaders and parents, *"If any, which of the following do you think are the primary reasons why some children leave their Christian faith by the time they become adults?"* Of the 14 options listed, children's ministry leaders selected, "Their parents/guardians did not model discipleship to them" as the leading selection (49%). Parents on the other hand selected, "They never felt a sense of belonging at church" as their top selection (30%).[1]

This is interesting in that these two groups, children's ministry leaders and parents, appear to be pointing at each other. There seems to be a disagreement, and it's by a wide margin, too! One group seems to be saying, "you are responsible" and the other is saying, "no, you are responsible."

Going a step further, the third highest selection for children's ministry leaders was, "Their parents/guardians were not engaged enough in the church" (35%).[2] Children's ministry leaders seem to have concluded that parents are somewhat lacking when it comes to parental discipleship engagement.

It feels a bit like a stalemate. What are we to do with this?

### Influential but Less Engaged at Church

If you've been to a conference on reaching and discipling children the last couple of decades, you've likely seen something like this. There's an illustration with tennis balls of all one color in a clear jar that represent the number of hours in a year that parents have with kids...and then another jar filled with very few tennis balls of another color that represent the very few hours a year the church has with kids. What's the point? Parents have far more hours a year (i.e., way more tennis balls) to invest in their children than the church does. It's quite clever. It's a powerful visual reminder that the formation of our children is an endeavor of time invested. Parents really do have far more hours with children at their disposal.

In this same 2022 Barna Group study, we wanted to dig into this a bit. We asked, *"Realistically, who has the greatest influence on a child's spiritual development?"* To no surprise, "Parents/Guardians" was ranked in the top spot by both children's ministry leaders (90%) and parents (68%).[3] Study after study, continues to highlight this reality, that realistically, parents have the greatest opportunity to influence their children—even the spiritual development of their children.

Study after study continues to show that parents have tremendous potential to influence their kids! Yet when it comes to their participation within the children's ministry at church (helping form the faith of their own children), parents are less engaged. Check out these quick hits:

- When it comes to local church engagement, we asked children's ministry leaders, *"At your church, how engaged are each of the following in children's ministry?"* Parents fell near the bottom at 26 percent.[4]

- When asked, *"Do you feel that you have an adequate number of parents, guardians, or grandparent helpers in your ministry?"* Sixty-five percent of children's ministry leaders said "no" they do not have enough.[5]

- In the area of support, the question was asked, "As a children's ministry leader, I wish I were receiving more support from..." Parents/Guardians came in at the top selection at 69 percent.[6]

- In a 2015 study on Kidmin leadership in the local church, we were trying to get an understanding of ministry effectiveness and we stated, *"Please tell how clear you believe the vision and purpose for your church's children's ministry is to the following. Please answer using a 5-point scale where 1 is "Not Clear" and 5 is "Completely Clear."* Children's ministry leaders ranked clarity among parents at the bottom at 3.14.[7]

I've not seen a single study that seems to refute this idea that "parents are the primary influence over their kids." I'm a parent myself, and I know this to be true: parents are influential. Praise God for this! This is how He designed it (Deuteronomy 6:4–9).

The question is, what are parents doing with this influence? How are we stewarding our influence? From the data I've seen in other studies, and the data we've collected, the big idea seems to be this: Parents have the potential and capacity to have a huge spiritual impact on the lives of their kids, but many church-going parents are simply less engaged in the child discipleship process.

This one point characterizes the heart of the issue. In our 2014 gap analysis study, children's ministry leaders ranked, *"Developing a partnership with parents/caregivers to help them in discipleship of their kids"* at an "importance" level of 4.67. However, we rated our "performance" level (what we think we are actually experiencing or achieving) at 3.24.[8] Of all of the "gaps" in this study between importance and performance, this was the largest gap and the lowest performance score. Meaning, church leaders see this as their biggest pain point when it comes to children's ministry or family ministry.

When it comes to partnering with parents, the outcomes are simply not what we want them to be. Parents are wildly influential, yet there seems to be a lack of engagement in the child discipleship journey.

### When Kids Pastors Say "Equipping Parents" Oftentimes They Mean "Distributing Resources"

One of the findings that came across clearly in the 2022 research that was covered at length in chapter five is this: kids pastors wish they could spend more relational time equipping parents. Kids pastors believe this is the most effective way of equipping a parent to disciple their child. Yet, due to the overwhelming burden of administrative tasks, fewer hours get invested in relational, equipping ministry.

In this same 2022 study, we were trying to understand, *"Specifically, what are you doing to equip parents to help them disciple their children?"* By a wide margin of almost 30 percent, the number one choice was "Providing them with resources/materials" (83.75%).[9]

Check this out though, the next five responses were all relational in nature: teaching (55.76%), spending time together (55.30%), connecting parents with other parents (47.18%), counseling (42.21%), and training (30.7%).

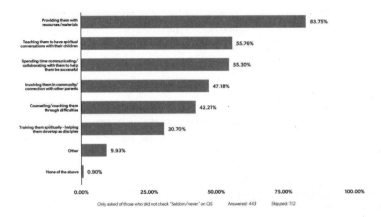

Providing them with resources/materials — 83.75%
Teaching them to have spiritual conversations with their children — 55.76%
Spending time communicating/collaborating with them to help them be successful — 55.30%
Involving them in community/connection with other parents — 47.18%
Counseling/coaching them through difficulties — 42.21%
Training them spiritually - helping them develop as disciples — 30.70%
Other — 9.93%
None of the above — 0.90%

0.00%   25.00%   50.00%   75.00%   100.00%

Only asked of those who did not check "Seldom/never" on Q5    Answered: 443    Skipped: 112

Providing resources to equip parents is clearly the church's current leading strategy. So, we wanted to know more about these resources. We asked, *"What resources/materials have you found to be the most helpful to parents as they disciple their children?"* Books was the leading response (27.76%), followed by Bible (14.56%), Take-home resources (14.29%), Devotions (9.7%), and surprisingly, Podcasts ranked lowest at only 6.2 percent.[10]

We then wanted to know to what degree the resources were being used and engaged by parents? The two leading responses were "Sometimes" (55.53%) and "I don't know" (14.82%).[11] A non-verbal gesture to represent this data would be a shrug of the shoulders.

There is actually an interesting and hopeful story here. Kids' pastors so desperately *want* to spend relational time equipping parents. Yet, due to our current map of administrative-heavy children's ministry (a symptom of the church growth model), the most efficient way for us to "equip" is to distribute a resource to parents. Kids pastors long to get more time with parents over a cup of coffee or doing discipleship training in a small group, but we are not sure how. So we do the best thing we know to do, which is to put quality equipping resources into the hands of parents, but we're not sure to what degree they are using them.

What are we to make of this?

### What's Most Effective in Equipping Parents? Relationships and Uncertainty

In this same 2022 study, we came across something surprising. When asking, *"What has been most effective/successful in helping parents disciple their children?*" I was not at all surprised that five of the top seven response were "relational" in nature. Conversation led the way at 21.08 percent, followed by mentoring/discipleship, teaching/classes, community/support, and encouragement.[12] What was so surprising is that "I don't know" or "not sure" came in as the second leading response.

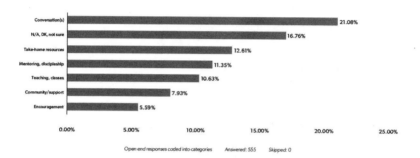

| | |
|---|---|
| Conversation(s) | 21.08% |
| N/A, DK, not sure | 16.76% |
| Take-home resources | 12.61% |
| Mentoring, discipleship | 11.35% |
| Teaching, classes | 10.63% |
| Community/support | 7.93% |
| Encouragement | 5.59% |

Open end responses coded into categories     Answered: 555     Skipped: 0

It's important to note that this was an "open ended" question, and right at the top in the second spot, there's a genuine sense of "Hmm. I really don't know what's most effective at equipping parents." Knowing all we know about "Parents and the Church" conversation, I genuinely don't think the data means "I'm clueless…I don't have any idea." It's far more likely to represent something more akin to "You know, we've tried several things and we have not figured this out yet." I'm guessing that what we are seeing here is more about exasperation and exhaustion and less about cluelessness.

The church knows if you want to be effective at equipping parents, you've got to be relational. We also have a sense of uncertainty about the whole thing.

### There's a Direct Connection Between "Time" and "Parents"

I love being a parent. Apart from being a husband, being a dad is my greatest joy as I walk this earth. There's just nothing quite like that feeling when I watch one of my sons achieve a long-labored-for-goal or when they simply walk in the door at the end of the day and give me a hug. These kids! We are just so proud of them, and our hearts burst with love for the children God entrusts to us.

Yet…

The heartache. Being a parent has also been the most exhausting work I've ever been a part of. It can be filled with grief, disappointment, pain, and hardship. Parenting is a lifetime journey of seemingly unending emotional highs and lows threaded together by the daily mundane.

Parenting is a gift, a burden, and a work of love.

Deuteronomy 6:4–9 says,

> *Hear, O Israel: The L*ORD *our God, the L*ORD *is one.*
> *You shall love the L*ORD *your God with all your heart and with*
> *all your soul and with all your might.*
> *And these words that I command you today shall be on your heart.*
> *You shall teach them diligently to your children,*
> *and shall talk of them when you sit in your house,*
> *and when you walk by the way, and when you lie down, and when you rise.*
> *You shall bind them as a sign on your hand,*
> *and they shall be as frontlets between your eyes.*
> *You shall write them on the doorposts of your house and on your gates* (ESV).

These are words that lead to life. These words are *the* way. They are the blueprint and parenting manual for how we pass the faith of Jesus Christ down from one generation to the next and to the next. This is one of the most beautiful passages in all of Scripture. As heavily invested parents and as church leaders, we long for every parent in our church community to live out this special passage of the Bible.

Yet, as we engage the parents in our church community, we encounter not-gonna-happen parents, less-engaged parents, and occasional parents. We can get frustrated by the lack of child discipleship engagement. On top of all of that, the ministry/work schedule for church leaders is wired mostly for administrative tasks, not for relational equipping. Something has to change.

We know there's a direct connection between relational equipping and parents, and this takes *time*. It takes time to meet a parent for coffee, breakfast, or lunch. It takes time to host a group of parents around a table for discussion.

There's a direct connection between "time" and "parents." If we want to see a change in parents discipling their kids, our ministry will likely need to look a lot more like Jesus' ministry: relational, discipling, mentoring, training, and equipping.

Let's go back to our question at the beginning of this chapter: What if churches formed a true partnership with parents that equips them to disciple their kids based on their capacities and capabilities? What could this look like?

To accomplish this, we need to rewire our weekly schedules (time). This will give church leaders just a bit more capacity to have more time to invest in discovering where parents are on their journey (or to equip others who can help in this process) so we can know how to inspire and equip them to become disciple-making parents. And for kids who live in not-gonna-happen kind of homes, the church will be a place of loving, caring, adult disciple-makers who maximize every moment possible to form the faith of these precious children. This is the kind of church families are looking for...this is the future of the church.

**Discussion Questions:**

1. What's the connection between "time" and "parents"? Discuss this as a team/group.
2. What one change can we make in our schedule to maximize relational investment in equipping and training parents for transformational impact?

**Endnotes**

[1] Research Project Seven, 35.

[2] Research Project Seven, 35.

[3] Research Project Seven, 57.

[4] Research Project Seven, 52.

[5] Research Project Seven, 52.

[6] Research Project Seven, 54.

[7] Research Project Three commissioned by Awana, *5by5 Research Agency* (Nashville, 5by5 Research Agency, 2015), 10.

[8] Research Project Two, 10.

[9] Research Project Eight, 112.

[10] Research Project Eight, 113.

[11] Research Project Eight, 114.

[12] Research Project Eight, 115.

CHAPTER 8

# METRICS

## Children's Ministry Leaders Find It Difficult to Measure and Evaluate Our Effectiveness

---

**If a lasting faith is our primary objective, what if we had a better understanding of the key metrics of faith formation in our children?**

Jux·ta·po·si·tion: the fact of two things being seen or placed close together with contrasting effect.

Juxtaposition is the first 50 cent word I remember learning as a young adult. I was so proud of myself—dropping the word juxtaposition into every conversation possible. Within the world of "child discipleship," I find the following juxtaposition to be worthy of our consideration.

| Christian Parents and church leaders alike agree there is nothing more important than the faith formation of our children. | Yet | We have very little (if any) sense of what key metrics to track, evaluate, or assess to help us form the faith of our children. |
| --- | --- | --- |

Forming the faith of children has been the chief investment of my life. Not just mine, but Katie's (my wife), too. We have invested significantly in discipling our own two sons. In addition, in ministry, we have spent the past 20 years in pursuit of the question, "What is it the church does that's most known to lead to lasting faith in children?" The pursuit of answering this question has been our life's central work.

Throughout this journey, a child discipleship think-tank community formed along the way. As this community has journeyed together, two key questions emerged. The first one was, *"What if we could change the language from 'children's ministry' to 'child discipleship'?"* As you likely know, children's ministry is a good term, yet it's a broad term with various meanings. Some of the efforts of children's ministry are more fruitful in reaching kids with the gospel and forming them as young disciples. Other efforts, not as much. Children's ministry is like a broad spectrum—a general descriptive term—a broad swath of various methodologies and purposes. Child discipleship, however, is focused. It's intentional. It's a mission built from Scripture and ancient objectives. We can extract child discipleship straight from the pages of the Gospels and build our ministries around it in accordance with the Great Commission.

To God be the glory, we have seen this vocabulary transformation begin to take place in our lifetime! More and more children's pastors are changing their titles from "Children's Ministry Pastor" to "Child Discipleship Pastor." More and more churches are using the term "child discipleship" interchangeably with the term "children's ministry." I see this as not only good, but necessary for the future.

Why is this so necessary? In the increasingly secularized, post-Christian West (like in the U.S. and in Europe), we need greater intentionality, not less. We need increased focus, not less. Again, consider reading: Kinnaman and Matlock, *Faith for Exiles: 5 Ways for a New Generation to Follow Jesus in a Digital Babylon.*[1] It's been said, if you can change the language, you can change the culture. In this instance, this is a good use of language change. We need increased focus and greater gospel intentionality in our secular age. In light of the increased and aggressive secularization in our culture, if we fail to increase our focus on child discipleship, we will see a continued drop in the resiliency of the faith of the next generation.

Which brings me to the second question that has emerged out of the child discipleship think-tank, and it's the central question of this chapter: *"What if we had a better understanding of the key metrics to track and evaluate the faith formation of our children?"*

I have saved this chapter for last because I have an audacious conviction that I believe deep, deep down to my bones. Here it is: I believe in the year 2050, children's ministry will look different from today.

You may be thinking, *"Well of course it will, that's over 25 years from now! Time and technology will change things."* But the reason for this change will not be simply the duration of years between now and then. To further emphasize the point, the way we are doing children's ministry today, minus some technological advancements, is not all that *objectively* different from the year 2000 (large group + small group format), and that was 23 years from the moment I'm striking this keyboard. So, if children's ministry hasn't objectively changed all that much in the past two decades, why the anticipated shift in the next 25 years? There are more nuanced reasons for the change I believe is coming, and here are the two primary reasons I see:

1. **Cultural Formation**: The church community is going to have to functionally understand that secularism is here and it's not going away. We need to come to grips with the fact that we live in a *Babylonian* type of context (as compared to a Jerusalem context). We are quite likely going to be raising our children *not* from a position of cultural power, but from the humble cultural margins. We should *expect* that secularism and post-Christian culture may become increasingly hostile and aggressive and it is not likely to relent. Therefore, for Bible believing, convictional Christ-followers who understand that our goal is to form children with lasting faith, we are quite likely to let go of the lesser things of children's ministry in exchange for the most fruitful primary factors known to influence a resilient, biblical faith in Jesus Christ. This is what's called *counter formation* or child discipleship—and it's filled with hope for the future!

2. **Counter Formation**: Earlier in this book, I referenced the way Jesus taught when He said, *"You have heard it said...but I tell you..."* What Jesus was doing when He spoke like this was a type of "counter formation." Jesus was essentially saying something akin to, *"Dominant culture is trying to tell you...but I am telling you to be formed in Me in a way that runs counter to the ways of this world..."* Discipleship, or child discipleship, is a type of formation that runs counter to the ways of this world. To God be the glory, thanks to the Bible and to modern research, we *do* have a grasp on the primary factors that are most known to form lasting faith in children (and we've discussed some of them in the previous chapters of this book). The Christ-following, Bible-believing parent of the future is going to be far less concerned about how entertaining our church children's ministries are, and is going to be far more concerned about *"How can you help me form lasting faith in my child in the midst of our highly secular culture?"* This shift is already beginning to take place now and is likely to become more and more evident in the years ahead.

In this final chapter (about metrics), the ultimate metric parents and pastors should be concerned about is the metric of "lasting faith" (covered in Chapter 1). Kids and young people who trust Christ as Savior and remain in faithful discipleship to Jesus Christ into young adulthood and beyond is what we are after. However, to realize that sort of *outcomes metric* often takes a couple of decades. Therefore, the job of the parent, pastor, or church leader is to develop a set of *key metrics* that are most known to shape and influence the lasting faith of our children. This is precisely why I'm asking in this chapter, "What if we had a better understanding of the key metrics of faith formation in our children?"

## Child Discipleship Is the Fearless, Hope-Filled, Joyful, Future of the Church

When you step back and look at all the endeavors of the local church, no other ministry is more dynamic, fruitful, hopeful, and rapidly growing than child discipleship. Kids are like sponges and are growing at a fast clip! Of all the areas of local church and family ministry one could invest in, none will yield greater spiritual harvest than investing in those from birth–14. For pastors, parents, volunteers, coaches, teachers, mentors, and grandparents, child discipleship is where it's at!

As those who care to shape and influence the faith of our children, we are not wondering around aimlessly. Because of what we know from the Bible, *and* because of what we know from modern research, the primary factors that form lasting faith in children *can* be understood. With this as a baseline understanding, I'm encouraged that we—this generation of seminary students, this era of the church leaders and parents—can now begin to collaborate and form a refined set of key *metrics* to help maximize how we disciple our children most fruitfully and faithfully in the secular age.

A clear grasp on the primary factors that form child disciples (and the key metrics within these areas) will reshape the future of children's ministry and will catapult the church community toward increased child discipleship fruitfulness. This excites me and is what I want to give my life to. I can't wait to see what type of collaboration and innovation emerges from leaders like you in the decades ahead as we continue to discover the key metrics that are most likely to influence the faith formation of our children.

## A Brief Word About the Importance of Metrics

Both of my sons are currently in college (senior and sophomore). With our oldest, when we ventured into the college search process, I was struck by the data each of the colleges were able to share with us as a prospective family: graduation rate per program, GPA per program, job placement rates per program, program national rankings, and a long list of other insightful metrics. Depending upon the seriousness and competitiveness of the child or the family, this data is a game changer in guiding a young adult toward the best college or university for him or her.

Yet I found myself back at that word, juxtaposition, once again as I thought about forming a resilient, biblical faith in our children. Why is it that colleges and universities have identified and can track key metrics to help our young people make their best higher education selection, but most local churches haven't identified primary metrics to maximize the faith formation of our children? If influencing, shaping, and forming the faith of our children is one of the most important aspects of parenting and local church ministry, it seems we have an unprecedented opportunity to increase our faithfulness and fruitfulness in the gospel with the next generation through a clearer understanding of which metrics are most known to shape a child's faith in Jesus.

So, why metrics? What's so important about metrics?

In Luke 14:28, Jesus asked, "Who builds a tower without first counting the cost?" In other words, if you want the final outcome of a completed structure, what are the key steps, materials, processes, and resources involved? And are you really up to the task? Each one of those "steps, materials, processes, and resources" are a type of metric: This many 2x4s, this many hammers and nails, the number of architects, the number of project managers, this many laborers, that much money, and so-on-and-so-forth. These are the key metrics you better have a firm grasp on if you want this project to have a successful outcome.

In a passage referenced earlier, Jesus said, "Therefore everyone who hears these words of mine and puts them into practice is like a wise man who built his house on the rock" (Matthew 7:24, NIV). In other words, if you want the *outcome* of a secure, sure, solid, stable life that resembles a house built on a rock, then *do these things* I have just told you. The teachings Jesus shared with His listeners about marriage, anger, lust, fasting, trusting God to provide, and loving your neighbor...these are the key metrics and action steps to pay attention to in order to build a life that is as solid as a house fortified upon a rock. Many will not choose this plan but will choose to ignore the practices of Jesus, meriting the outcome of an unstable foundation that ends in disaster. Yet, the few who do pay attention to these metrics will discover the outcome of abundant life in Jesus Christ.

I've had a high metabolism my entire life...until I hit my upper 40s. Ugh. To be honest, until recently, I felt invincible and really never had to give much thought to the health of my body. Those days have now passed. I'm just now joining the rest of planet earth and realizing that if I want the outcome of a healthy weight range then there are certain metrics that matter: calories, steps a day, minutes of cardio workout a week, stretching, ounces of water a day, breathing exercises, foods to avoid, foods to consume, and a long list of other things I'm now paying attention to (thank you Katie, Mike, and Kevin).

Inside our organization we use these two terms:

Drivers  →  Outcomes

In our context at Awana, *drivers* (like calories, exercise, water, and food) are the fewest number of key actions or metrics per ministry or program we *can* control that have the highest impact on shaping the outcome (like weight loss). We can't immediately command that the outcome change, but we can *influence* it by focusing on the drivers we can control. Both drivers and outcomes are metrics—just different types of metrics. Drivers are metrics you can immediately control. Outcomes are metrics you can only influence through the use of drivers.

Just like a college knows their key metrics to track to understand how to influence their effectiveness per program; and just like a construction builder knows what key metrics to track to successfully build a structure; and just like I now know what lead drivers to pay attention to maximize the health of my body; what if the church knew what the fewest numbers of lead drivers were that tend to influence (not control) lasting faith in children? If we knew what those lead drivers were, would we pay more attention to those drivers? Would we place more emphasis on those areas to maximize our fruitfulness and gospel impact?

Let's go back to the central question we are asking in this book, the question first mentioned in the introduction, which asks:

**What is it the church does that leads to lasting faith in children?**

This question is all about drivers and outcomes.

- **Drivers** – "What is it the church does…"
  - ○ The key *behaviors* loving, caring adults *can immediately do to influence*, shape, and form a child's faith.
- **Outcomes** – "…that leads to lasting faith in children?"

  - ○ The *outcomes* in a child's life as a *result of the influence* of a loving, caring, adult child disciple-maker and the work of the Holy Spirit.

As we discussed in chapters 2 and 3, a wise church community will build a church culture where loving, caring adults connect with kids consistently in a highly relational way and they create environments at church and home that are consistently Scripture rich. (These are *drivers*—key behaviors that we can immediately and implement.) These drivers don't guarantee lasting faith in children, but they do give all kids in our church community the greatest opportunity and probability to become a thriving disciple of Jesus Christ.

Metrics matter. Because key metrics (drivers) can influence outcomes.

### Defining Success Requires Metrics

In the same research project referenced in Chapter 1 around "defining success," we also asked a different question, *"How would you rate the overall success and impact of the children's ministry at your church? Please answer using a 5-point scale where 1 is not at all successful and 5 is very successful."*[2]

I'm curious, have you ever used an app like *Yelp* to help you choose a restaurant? Or *Amazon* to help you purchase a book? I ask because, whenever I'm looking for a place to take Katie out to dinner, if I see a score like 3.6, I'm sure to keep moving and look for a better rating of 4.0 or above. If I see a book that scores at 3.6, I want to read the reviews to understand why it's scoring so low.

What does 3.65 mean?

In the context of the question, *"How would you rate the overall success and impact of the children's ministry at your church?"* A 3.65 percent simply means we are not meeting our own expectations. Our "overall success and impact" within our children's ministry is simply not where we want it to be. If we wouldn't take our spouse out to dinner at a 3.6 restaurant, we are certainly not happy with an overall children's ministry success rate of 3.65. We find ourselves, deep down inside, longing for something better.

In this same survey, the very next question we asked was, *"Specifically, why don't you view your children's ministry as more successful?"*[3] Consistent with much of the other research we have commissioned, it all comes down to relationships. The three top reasons that children's ministry leaders tend to view their ministries as less successful are relational in nature:

And the converse is also true. We then asked, *"Specifically, why do you view your children's ministry so successfully?"*[4] The top three responses were as follows:

So, what do children's ministry leaders tend to think the bottom line is when it comes to a successful children's ministry? It's this: when kids are learning and we have loving, caring adults engaging at church and at home, we are working our way toward success. I happen to agree. This is a decent starting point when painting a general picture of baseline success. As a community, however, we are currently rating ourselves at a score of 3.65. That's not a restaurant we want to eat at. We are not quite where we want to be yet...we are yearning for something more. We need to go a step further.

We realize that to define something as "successful," metrics *are required*. The Children's Ministry community is just not quite certain how to do this well within the area of child faith formation. Even the response to the question above such as "Kids are learning" is a bit arbitrary. How do we know the kids are learning? We could even ask, what *kind* of volunteers do we have? And how effectively are they engaging the kids? There's a level of specificity that seems to be lacking because it can be difficult to track and evaluate. Which is precisely the next section we will tackle.

## Children's Ministry Seems Difficult to Evaluate

In this same 2019 study, we asked, *"How carefully are you and your team evaluating, tracking, and measuring the success and impact of the overall children's ministry at your church? Please answer using a 5-point scale where 1 is poor and 5 is excellent."*[5]

| | | 2.99% | | |
|---|---|---|---|---|
| 1 | 2 | 3 | 4 | 5 |

I genuinely view this as one of the most insightful findings in my 10+ years of commissioning research projects. Parents, pastors, and children's ministry leaders alike agree that forming the faith of our children is one of the most important aspects of the church ministry at large (again, look at what was covered in Chapter 1). However, when it comes to "tracking and measuring" our "success and impact" we are giving it a shrug of the shoulders. A score of 2.99 means, we just don't know.

> When it comes to finding a way of tracking, measuring,
> and evaluating the very thing that is the most important thing
> to us in all the universe we don't have a very good response
> in terms of how well we are doing.

The Barna Group found the same thing to be true in our 2022 study *Children's Ministry in a New Reality* when we asked, *"How easy or difficult is it to evaluate the impact children's ministry is having on children?"* Almost half, 48 percent, said evaluating the impact of children's ministry was somewhat difficult or very difficult.[6] Once again, right at that half-way mark—split right down the middle—we tend to find it difficult to evaluate the impact of children's ministry. There's a sense of "We're just not sure."

In 2019, when we then asked, *"Why are you not more effective in evaluating/measuring/validating success and impact?"* the two leading, open-ended responses were that it's "Difficult to Evaluate" (25.82%) and the fact that there is "No Tool/Instrument" to evaluate (22.54%). This also came through in the qualitative focus groups where we heard these comments from children's ministry leaders:

- *"We don't have a tracking tool for this."*
- *"We haven't defined specific markers to look for and track as far as impact. At this point, it is primarily anecdotal evidence."*
- *"We are unsure of available resource to assess and evaluate."*
- *"We don't have a tool in place to specifically measure our impact just yet."*
- *"We are still trying to find the systems and processes that works best."*[7]

Notice the words, "We don't have a tool for this," and "We are unsure," and "still trying to find the systems." What do you see here? If we were to give it a number, once again it's that 2.99 percent. It's the 48 percent mark. It's the shrug of the shoulders. It's, "I just don't know."

Let's go a step further. In this same study, we also asked, "What are the specific ways you do evaluate/measure/validate success and impact?" and the two overwhelmingly leading responses were "Analyze Subjectively" (40.34%) and "Attendance" (38.66%). So as a community, when we *do* evaluate the effectiveness of our children's ministries, it tends to come down to a subjective evaluation (which will vary from person to person and church to church) and if children are showing up.

Imagine being a cross-country runner but having no grasp on your metrics, your timing, or your pacing. Once you were halfway through the race, how would you know how to adjust to make up your time. Quite simply, you wouldn't. It would be a guessing game. A shrug of the shoulders.

But does it have to be this way? It doesn't. Because of what we can learn by observing how Jesus made disciples in the Gospels and the distilling down of modern child faith formation research, we can begin to develop key metrics within the three primary areas most known to form lasting faith in children.

**The Three Most Important Metrics to Shape the Future of the Church**

Multiple times throughout this book, including in this chapter, I have referenced the singular question that has been at the center of our research, and it's this: *"What is it the church does that leads to lasting faith in children?"*

Now, when I say "the church" in this sentence, hopefully at this point it's abundantly clear that what I mean by *church* is the broader church community: pastors, parents, children's ministry leaders, volunteers, teachers, grandparents, coaches, mentors, congregants, aunts, and uncles. From the perspective of the child, "the church" is the community of people who can help that child know, love, and serve Jesus Christ for a lifetime. The church is the community of potential child disciple-makers.

Parents are a central part of this child disciple-making community. According to the Bible, they are most responsible to disciple their children (Deuteronomy 6:4–9). In a similar way, as a parent I was the person most responsible for my two sons' education. When it came to certain aspects of their education—say, Chemistry or Physics or Calculus—I called in the experts. I am more of an art, words, literature, P.E. kind of guy. When it comes to math and sciences, I'm simply in over my head. Thankfully, the boys had other teachers in their lives who could help fill in those gaps. When it comes to child discipleship, it's much the same way. Parents have a crucial role, but no individual parent (or two parents for that matter) is going to be able to fulfill all of the voids, gaps, and needs in the spiritual life of a child. This is one of the structures of grace God has given us with the church community.

In chapter 7, we discussed "Higher-Capacity Parents." We defined this group as parents who are "highly engaged in discipling their own children. They are disciples of Jesus themselves, and they are intentional about discipling their own children." Even this group of all-in high-flying kind of parents needs other people to surround the life of their child. They need other loving, caring adults who will reinforce the web of Christlike community. This is what the church is all about. Then there's the other end of the spectrum with the Not-Gonna-Happen parents. We said about this group, "there are some parents who simply will not engage in discipling their own children." This group of parents is almost entirely relying upon the structure of grace of the broader church community to disciple their children. This may not be ideal, and it may not even be what God intends, yet it's the reality that a high percentage of children find themselves in.

This is precisely why God gave us the church and qualified pastors to teach, lead, and shepherd us. Parents need pastors and local church leaders (much like I needed someone else to help my sons with Chemistry class) to equip them for the work of child discipleship (Ephesians 4:12; Matthew 28:18–20). Discipling children has never been a walk in the park, and in today's rapidly changing and hostile culture, parents now need equipping more than ever. Trained, loving, caring pastors can be of tremendous value to give parents equipping and insight as to *how* to disciple their children at home. Parents need pastors to give them discipleship training. Parents need Small Group leaders, Large Group teachers, Sunday School teachers, Kids' Pastors, mentors, church volunteers, and the church community at large.

Here's where we find ourselves:

> Parents are the most responsible and have the most access (hours in a week) to disciple their children, but often are less equipped in knowing how to disciple their kids.

> Church leaders are often the most trained and equipped in knowing how to disciple children but have the least amount of hourly access to the children in their church community.

For the sake of children, this is the beauty of the local church community— God's structure of grace for us. For kids who live in a Not-Gonna-Happen kind of home, the church steps up and leans in! The church says, "We see you child. We know you; you belong here, we love you, and we will take on the responsibility of loving you to Jesus, teaching you the Bible, reaching you with the Gospel, and walking beside you as your disciple-maker." In the case of the child who lives in a home where the parents are more engaged in the discipleship journey, the parents can benefit greatly from being discipled, mentored, trained, and equipped on how to be a disciple and how to disciple their own children at home.

Parents are responsible. Yes, and...

Parents need pastors and kids' pastors to equip and train them.

Parents also need the broader church community to participate in the cultivation of the faith of their children.

So, back to the question at hand: *"What is it the church does that leads to lasting faith in children?"* When we take all the research of the past decade and boil it down, we find three factors that have the highest impact on forming the faith of our children. Those three factors are:

> **BELONG** – Highly relational ministry led by loving, caring adults.

> **BELIEVE** – Deeply scriptural ministry rooted in gospel and the truth of God's Word in order that kids may know, love, and serve Jesus Christ.

> **BECOME** – Truly experiential ministry designed to help kids navigate a changing culture, experience God's presence, and walk in the ways of Jesus.[8]

In one sentence it looks like this: *Child Discipleship* is a process designed to form lasting faith by helping kids **belong** to God and His Kingdom, **believe** in Jesus Christ as Lord and Savior, and to **become** like Jesus and walk in His ways through the power of the Holy Spirit.

The aim of child discipleship is to ensure that a child's environment is highly relational, deeply Scriptural, and truly experiential—all happening simultaneously in the life of a child. This is the essence of fruitful, timeless, effective child discipleship. No formulas. No false guarantees. Just the distilling of the best of ancient church practices of the past 2000 years, rooted in the faithfulness of what we can observe about discipleship in the Bible.

At Awana, we call these three primary practices "3B" Child Discipleship. A couple of things to point out: 1) Remember, these are answering the question, "What is it the church does...." Therefore, these 3Bs inform and describe *what* we *do* and *how* we can *do* it—our *behaviors* that we as adult disciple-makers do to influence the faith of the children in our lives. 2) Notice the careful way these definitions are worded. They are not "local church" centric, nor are they "home" centric. These 3B definitions can be applied anywhere: church, home, coaches, teachers, grandparents, out and about, etc. They inform how the church community goes about engaging children. They help you and me understand that we need to be highly relational in how we engage children— deeply scriptural in the way we engage children—and making sure that kids have ways to truly experience the living-out of their faith for Christ in today's world.

So what does all of this have to do with metrics?

If we have discovered that adult disciple-makers need to focus on embodying Belonging, Believing, and Becoming to cultivate lasting faith in children, then we have identified the behaviors from adult disciple-makers that we need to be measuring. These are the three primary areas we need to be paying attention to at church, and at home. For a moment, think about the comments some of our research respondents said about metrics earlier in this chapter:

"We haven't defined specific markers to look for and track as far as impact. At this point, it is primarily anecdotal evidence."

"We don't have a tool in place to specifically measure our impact just yet."

"We don't have a tracking tool for this."

We may not have a tracking tool for this just yet, but we *have* identified the key markers.

What if there was a tool to help us track and evaluate how well we exude "Belonging" to the children in our ministries or in our homes? A tool to help us understand our relational effectiveness? What if there was an instrument to assess our Scripture engagement with children? Or what if there was a survey to give us insight on how well we are doing at creating an experiential environment for the kids in our lives?

The more insight we can gain on how we exude the key behaviors (metrics) around Belonging, Believing, and Becoming in the lives of children, the more we can shape the future of the church.

## A Final Exercise: Key Metrics Within Each of the 3Bs

The 3Bs are the primary factors embodied by adult disciple-makers to cultivate lasting faith in children. Each one of the 3Bs is a description of the embodiment, behaviors, and attitudes of adult disciple-makers—adults who commit to being highly relational, deeply scriptural, and truly experiential in how they approach the faith formation of the kids in their lives (at church and at home).

Earlier in this chapter, I stated that I see a framework for where the church needs to go based on our research and there is a significant need for dialogue and collaboration among all of us. To be abundantly clear, this framework is 3B child discipleship. The following exercise offers an opportunity for pastors, church leaders, parents, and volunteers to begin the collaborative process of understanding what key behaviors we put into action that can become the metrics of the future.

This exercise will be most effective if done with a team or a small group. Even if done alone, that's a great start. But if you have the opportunity to do this exercise with your church leadership team or a small group it will go further in helping you reshape the culture of child discipleship cultivation in your community. Either way, 2 points for getting the ball rolling.

Using the 3B definitions above in this chapter, build a *Mind Map* for Belong, Believe, and Become. (For examples, search Mind Map on Google Images.) As you build your mind map for each B, ask yourself, what behaviors do I/we do that can help exude this B? What attitudes or insights will help us become more effective at this B? As you build out your mind map, be sure to stay away from generalities, and to look for specific actions, behaviors, and attitudes you can pinpoint. Here are some examples:

- **For Belong** (Highly relational) – Greet each child by name, look children in the eye when speaking to them, put the mobile phones away, ask kids questions about their interests, etc.

- **For Believe** (Deeply scriptural) – Use a physical Bible (book) instead of a mobile device, read the Bible aloud together, sing Scripture music together, teach kids how to read the Bible or memorize Scripture on their own, etc.

- **For Become** (Truly experiential) – Model with kids how to pray, engage kids in conversation about what's happening at their schools and with their friends, give kids opportunities to serve, model for kids specific ways to live out their faith, etc.

**BELONG Mind Map:** Highly relational ministry led by loving, caring adults.

Keeping in mind the core question, "What is it the church ***does*** that's most known to lead to lasting faith in children?" Be sure to list actions and attitudes that adults can *do* to embody the definition and description of *Belong*.

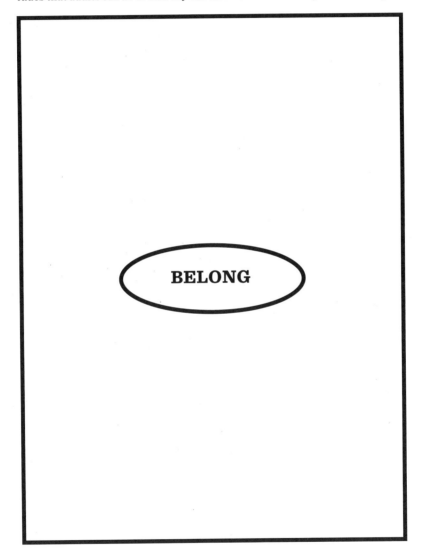

**BELIEVE Mind Map:** Deeply scriptural ministry rooted in gospel and the truth of God's Word in order that kids may know, love, and serve Jesus Christ.

Keeping in mind the core question, "What is it the church *does* that's most known to lead to lasting faith in children?" Be sure to list actions and attitudes that adults can *do* to embody the definition and description of *Believe*.

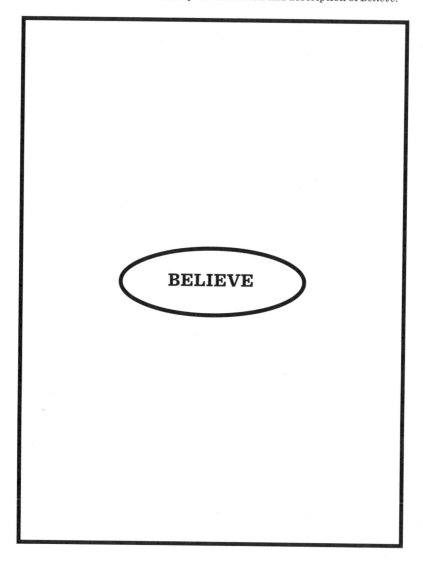

**BECOME Mind Map:** Truly experiential ministry designed to help kids navigate a changing culture, experience God's presence, and walk in the ways of Jesus.[9]

Keeping in mind the core question, "What is it the church **does** that's most known to lead to lasting faith in children?" Be sure to list actions and attitudes that adults can *do* to embody the definition and description of *Become*.

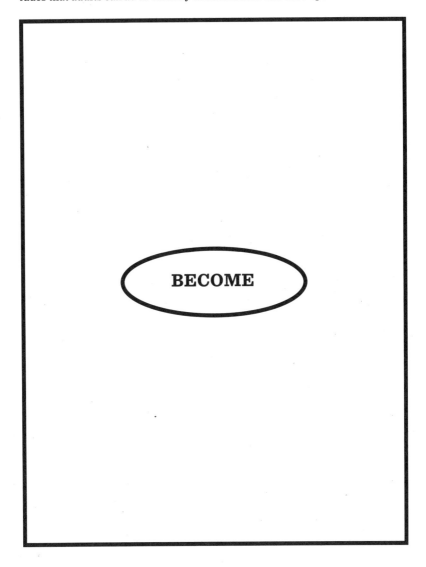

**SHARE YOUR RESULTS WITH US!**

Would you like to share your top 3–5 ideas within each B with me? I'd love to see what you came up with! Email me at communications@awana.org. We will share the results at ChildDiscipleship.com. I look forward to sharing with you.

**Discussion Questions:**

1. Do you think parents and churches should have a clear grasp on the primary areas to focus on in order to cultivate lasting faith in children?

2. When it comes to the faith cultivation of children in your community or home, what metrics do you currently track, assess, and evaluate? Do you think you are paying attention to the most important metrics?

3. When you think about Belong (highly relational), Believe (deeply scriptural), and Become (truly experiential), how do those key areas of faith formation resonate with you? Do they ring true to your own study and experience?

4. By using the 3B Mind Map exercise, what are the top 3–5 ideas you came up with for each B? How could you begin to use those ideas to create a new set of metrics to shape the faith of the kids in your community?

**Endnotes**

[1] Kinnaman and Matlock, *Faith for Exiles.*

[2] Research Project Four, 54.

[3] Research Project Four, 55.

[4] Research Project Four, 56.

[5] Research Project Four, 59.

[6] Research Project Seven, 20.

[7] Research Project Four, 37.

[8] Bell, Markins, and Handler, *Resilient,* 171.

[9] Bell, Markins, and Handler, *Resilient,* 171.

# LETTER TO YOUR PASTOR

I wish we could get to know each other and chat about the insights covered in this book. It would be nice if you and I were sitting across the table together over a cup of coffee (hmm, maybe afternoon tea...or for some your diet drink of choice). I would love nothing more than to hear your thoughts. What insight in this book resonated with you? What caused you to get defensive? What broke your heart? What got you excited about the future? Even as I wrote these chapters, I went thought all these thoughts and emotions, and more.

For most readers, I likely don't know you. I hope to meet you one day, but I don't know you personally. I'd like to know, what do you do? Are you a concerned parent? A teacher or coach? A kid's pastor? Whomever you are, I know we share much in common, and one of the things we share in common is our love for the local church and a deep appreciation for those who lead our churches—our pastors.

If this book resonated with you, you likely thought to yourself at some point, "Oh I wish my pastor could read this!" Pastors are busy. They have a big responsibility, and a lot on their mind and heart. Many pastors may not want to invest the time to read a 100-page book on children. You and I hope that more and more pastors would! But that may not happen in each local church community.

So, I've written a letter to your pastor. This is my gift to you, so you can give it to your pastor. If you think I've done a good job here of capturing your heart (and the essence of the insights in this book), I encourage you to tear it out and give it to your pastor. Go ahead. Rip it out! Type A's, go and get the scissors. Cut away, it's okay. Or you can download a copy at ChildDisciplship.com/foc-pastor-letter/ to print or email. I pray this is one small step in helping you shape the culture of your church to be one that forms the faith of our children.

Until we meet, or until we meet again.

*Matt M*

Matt Markins
Awana, President and CEO
mattm@awana.org

Dear Pastor,

I genuinely think you have the most important job on the planet. Not only that, but you also have one of the most difficult jobs in all of the earth. You continue to remain a faithful minister of the gospel because you sense a deep spiritual calling, you love Jesus Christ wholly, and you want to see others know, love, and serve Him for the rest of their lives.

Thank you. The world needs more pastors like *you*.

The ministry that I steward and lead has been around 73 years. We engage 5.6 million children in weekly child discipleship in 132 countries through 72,000 church partners. During that journey, we've learned a lot about what shapes lasting faith in children. I'd love to share with you briefly a few highlights you may find insightful based on your heart for the gospel and love for the local church.

In our ministry, we have a saying that goes like this: We are centered on the gospel, rooted in Scripture, and we will never move one inch off the Bible. In addition, over the past decade we've also invested significantly in *research*. As a matter of fact, the person who gave you this letter has been reading my book about child discipleship research—the chief insights we've learned about discipling kids, and why this matters in today's aggressive, secular culture.

We've been asking the question,

*"What is it the church does that leads to lasting faith in children?"*

I'd like to share with you why, after a decade of research, this is one of the most important questions that a lead pastor/senior pastor could be asking.

## We're Up Against a Deadline

As church leaders, we tend to look at the looming deadline to get students ready to go out into the world as disciples of Jesus Christ at age 18. The reality is, 18 is far too late.

We have high hopes that our young people will graduate high school, go out onto their college campuses, and be Christ's advocates in the world. But sadly, a high percentage of students become more formed by the very world we hope they will reach for Christ. Why is this? What's happening here? According to the Barna Group,

*"...a person's worldview is primarily shaped and is firmly in place*
*by the time someone reaches the age of 13."*[1]

Let's think about this together for a moment. Who is today's 13-year-old? Today's 13-year-old recently entered into your church's youth group. Two years prior to that, they were 11 years old and were graduating from your church's children's ministry. Three years before that they were eight years old and were right in the heart of your children's ministry—at the age when their worldview is being formed.

If most human beings' worldview is shaped and is firmly in place by the time they reach the age of 13, perhaps this is a more accurate picture of what's happening in our churches:

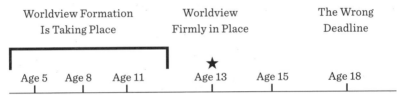

| Worldview Formation Is Taking Place | Worldview Firmly in Place | The Wrong Deadline |
|---|---|---|
| Age 5   Age 8   Age 11 | ★ Age 13   Age 15 | Age 18 |

In most churches, our entire system operates as if age 18 is the deadline for which we are aiming. The data, however, tells a different story. We're up against a deadline, and it's earlier than we thought. It's not 18, it's 13.

This means that what's happening prior to age 13 is some of the most power-ful work of the church. We call this, child discipleship. But the church is not the only entity aiming to *"disciple"* our children.

## The Fear of Cultural Formation And the Hope of Child Discipleship

You've likely read about the cultural shifts taking place in the West and spe-cifically in the U.S. Words like secularism, post-Christian culture, naturalism, hedonism, and transgenderism are no longer academic terms but pedestrian. These realities are no longer "out there" but they have become the dominant, mainstream culture of today. If our kids were fish, this is the water in which they are swimming (so to speak).

What do we call this? It's *Cultural Formation*. It's been said, it's not a matter of "Are our kids being discipled?" Rather, it's a matter of "Who or what is discipling our kids?" To be sure, cultural formation is a powerful force that's at work in our hyper digital, screen environments where kids have access to more information by the age of ten than previous generations experienced in their entire lifetime.

What can stand against such a powerful cultural force? The gospel can. Child discipleship can. We do not have to fear. The gospel is more powerful than the secular cultural forces. Our children need a resilient faith that will bend and flex, but not break under the weight of culture.

Can I give you some hopeful news? We've learned a lot about the primary factors most known to form lasting faith in children. The book this letter came from is filled with biblical and research-based insights on how to most fruitfully disciple today's kids! This is our most strategic investment in shaping the future of the church.

**The Church of 2050**

I once heard a pastor ask, "Are we adequately preparing today's kids to thrive in their faith in a world few of us can hardly comprehend?"

There is likely no one in your church who cares more deeply about the future of your church than you. If I may be so bold, child discipleship is the most fruitful work of the church. It's the most influential work of the church. But most pastors give it little brain space.

The most strategic way to shape the future of the church—in a future culture few of us can even wrap our minds around—is to invest in child discipleship.

There's so much we've learned about how to be more fruitful and effective with today's kids. You can read about it in this book. We also host training and dialogue-based events all over the country. Or you can email me at my email address below. I'd love to continue the conversation.

May God bless you as you shape the church of 2050.

Matt Markins
Awana, President and CEO
Author of *The Faith of Our Children: Eight Timely Research Insights for Discipling the Next Generation*
mattm@awana.org

**Endnote**

1 http://www.barna.com/research/barna-survey-examines-changes-in-worldview-among-christians-over-the-past-13-years/.

# ACKNOWLEDGMENTS

In Matthew 7:24–27, Jesus says that a "wise" man "hears" the words of His teaching and "puts them into practice." This is similar to what research teaches us. As wise Christ-followers, we posture our minds and hearts toward listening for wisdom and insight. To what end? Gospel transformation—to put what we learn into practice! Learning from research is gospel stewardship.

With this idea in mind, I didn't get here on my own. I'm indebted to a great number of people and am standing on the shoulders of faithful organizations and institutions.

I *thank* those who inspired our thinking. First and foremost, Jesus Christ our King who has opened my eyes to priceless insights (Matthew 13:44). I also thank: My ministry partner Katie Markins; William F. Meehan III and Kim Starky Jonker for their work *Engine of Impact* (Theory of Change); Jimmy Mellado of Compassion International (M.E.R.L); Barna Group; numerous friends in Christian higher education; the Children's Spirituality Summit; the Child Discipleship Forum community; our *Resilient* readership; the children's ministry leaders and pastors who dare to ask the hard questions; and various works by John Mark Comer, Mark Sayers, David Kinnaman, Mark Matlock, Gabe Lyons, Tony Evans, Kara Powell, Albert Mohler, Christian Smith, Francis Schaeffer, Darren Whitehead, Jon Tyson, Dallas Willard, George Barna, Dietrich Bonhoeffer, Pete Scazzero, Sean McDowell, Tim Keller, and Ed Stetzer.

I also thank our team who captured the vision and did the work: Mark McPeak, Mike Handler, Kevin White, Brian Rhodes, Ed Gossien, Steve Cohoon, Kevin Orris, Beth Bedoe, Chip Root, Sara Dudt, Ken Toeller, Kellie Bartley, Tim Sandvall, Colin Robinson, Yeli Acevedo, Tom Chilton, Alicia Tracy, Gajendra Tamang, Stephen Maphosah, Miguel Perez, Mark Campbell, Peter Mayberry, Dan Lovaglia, Casey Pontious, Norm Whitney, and the Awana Board of Directors.

Much of our research is funded by the generosity of our donors. You are true ministry partners. We are beyond grateful for you and we love you deeply. What could be more important than investing in forming the faith of our children?

# LIST OF RESEARCH
# PROJECTS AND
# RESEARCH METHODOLOGY

**Research Project One – Children's Ministry Effectiveness (5by5 Agency, 2013)**

Quantitative Methodology
- Survey
- Estimated Population...........300,000 evangelical churches in the U.S.
- Sample Size.............................376
- Margin of Error.......................+/– 5.05%

**Research Project Two – Children's Ministry Curriculum Choices (5by5 Agency, 2014)**

Quantitative Methodology
- Survey
- Estimated Population...........300,000 evangelical churches in the U.S.
- Sample Size.............................1,218
- Margin of Error.......................+/– 2.80%
- Audience: Full-time children's pastor/director (26.25%), part-time children's pastor/director (14.87%), volunteer children's ministry leader (24.74%), volunteer (small group leader, teacher, worker – 13.82%), Other (20.33%)
- Church Denomination: Non-denominational (32.98%), Southern Baptist (22.49%), Baptist (non-SBC – 14.92%), Assemblies of God (6.64%), Pentecostal (5.48%), Evangelical Free (5.01%), Methodist (3.96%), Charismatic (2.1%), Presbyterian (2.1%), Church of God (1.52%), Other (2.8%).
- Church Size: 100 or less (20.47%), 101 – 200 (24.65%), 201 – 500 (27.91%), 501 – 1,000 (14.65%), 1,001 – 3,000 (7.79%), 3,001 or more (4.53%)

Qualitative Methodology
- One Focus Group – Children's pastor, children's ministry directors, Awana ministry directors (Full-time and part-time)

**Research Project Three – Cross Functional Children's Ministry Leadership in the Local Church (5by5 Agency, 2015)**

Quantitative Methodology
- Survey
- Estimated Populatio ............ 300,000 evangelical churches in the U.S.
- Sample Size ............................ 444
- Margin of Error ...................... +/– 4.67%
- Audience: Full-time children's pastor/director (57.94%), part-time children's pastor/director (22.06%), volunteer children's ministry leader (20%)
- Church Denomination: Southern Baptist (22.06%), Non-denominational (18.24%), Baptist (non-SBC – 12.94%), Methodist (9.41%), Presbyterian (4.71%), Evangelical Free (3.24%), Church of Christ (2.94%), Assemblies of God (2.65%), Lutheran (1.18%), Other (22.63%).
- Church Size: 100 or less (9.14%), 101 – 200 (15.63%), 201 – 500 (31.27%), 501 – 1,000 (20.06%), 1,001 – 2,000 (13.57%), 2,001 or more (7.67%), 5,001 or more (2.65%)

**Research Project Four – Child Discipleship in the Local Church (5by5 Agency, 2019)**

Quantitative Methodology
- Survey
- Estimated Population ........... 1M Children's Ministry Decision Makers
- Sample Size ............................ 624
- Margin of Error ...................... +/– 3.92%
- Audience: Full-time children's pastor/director (25.32%), part-time children's pastor/director (16.51%), volunteer children's ministry leader (29.49), volunteers and other (28.68%).
- Church Denomination: Baptist (34.29%), Non-denominational (24.2%), Methodist (5.93%), Evangelical Free Church (5.45%), Others (30.13%)

- Church Size: 100 or less (21.47%), 101 – 200 (22.76%), 201 – 500 (30.13%), 501 – 1,000 (11.54%), 1,001 – 3,000 (11.22%), 3,001 or more (2.88%).

Qualitative Methodology
- Group 1 – Full-time Children's pastor/director of large and mega Baptist churches: 9 participants
- Group 2 – Full-time Children's pastor/director of large and mega non-denominational churches: 12 participants
- Group 3 – Mixture of Full-time Children's pastor/director from a variety of church sizes and denominations: 13 participants
- Group 4 – Mixture of Full-time, part-time, and volunteer Awana ministry leaders from a variety of church sizes and denominations: 16 participants

**Research Project Five – Children's Ministry Weekend Curriculum (5by5 Agency, 2019)**

- Not referenced in this book.

**Research Project Six – Awana Child Discipleship Impact Study: U.S. (Excellence in Giving, 2020)**

- Survey
- 1,065 18–74-year-olds
- 2.15% margin of error with a 95% confidence level
- Survey respondents represented 48 of 50 states
- The sample compared participants with less than one year of participation to more than ten years of participation to determine if the length of AWANA's intervention produced measurable differences in religious knowledge, attitudes, or practices.

**Research Project Seven – Resilient Child Discipleship/Children's Ministry in a New Reality (Barna Group, 2022)**

"This study included a set of quantitative online surveys.

The first survey interviewed 2,051 U.S. adults who attended church at least once in the last six months. They were surveyed online between June 11–July 6, 2021, through a national consumer research panel. Included within the sample of churched adults is an oversample of 1,021 parents with children between the ages of 5 and 14 years old. The data has been statistically weighted by age, gender, race/ethnicity, income, education, region, and parenting. The estimated margin of error is +/– 1.8%.

Additionally, Barna surveyed 600 U.S. Protestant church leaders who indicate they have decision-making responsibility for their church's children's ministry. Within this sample, 481 leaders are specifically on-staff children's pastors, on-staff youth pastors or volunteer children's leaders, and 119 leaders are senior pastors who don't have a children's ministry leader. For recruitment, Barna Group reached out to senior protestant pastors through Barna's Pastor Panel and asked them to forward the invitation to whomever is responsible for children's ministry in their church. The data has been statistically weighted by church size, region, and denomination. The estimated margin of error is +/– 2.5%."[2]

### Research Project Eight – How Children's Ministry Leaders Spend Their Time (5by5 Agency, 2022)

Quantitative Methodology
- Estimated Population...........1M Children's Ministry Decision Makers
- Sample Size.............................555
- Margin of Error......................+/– 4.16%
- Audience: Full-time children's pastor (39.5%), part-time children's pastor/director (23.6%), volunteer children's ministry leader (18.5), volunteers and other (18.4%).
- Denominational Affiliation: Baptist (34.6%), Non-denominational (26%), Others (39.4%)

Qualitative Methodology
- Group 1 – Church Size <200, 5+ years' experience: 7 participants
- Group 2 – Church Size 200 – 500, higher pastor engagement, 5+ years' experience: 5 participants
- Group 3 – Church Size 200 – 500, lower pastor engagement, 5+ years' experience: 11 participants
- Group 4 – Church Size >500, 5+ years' experience: 10 participants

**Research Project Nine – Awana Child Discipleship Impact Study: Africa & S.E. Asia (Excellence in Giving: 2023)**

- Not referenced in this book.

**Research Project Ten – The State of Midweek Children's Ministry (5by5 Agency, 2023)**

- Not completed by the time of the publishing of this book
- Not referenced in this book

**Research Project Eleven – Children's Ministry Effectiveness (5by5 Agency, 2023)**

- Not completed by the time of the publishing of this book
- Not referenced in this book

**Endnotes** ——————————————

[1] https://www.barna.com/research/barna-survey-examines-changes-in-worldview-among-christians-over-the-past-13-years/.

[2] Research Project Seven, 89.